BYTE ME!

Computing for the
Terminally Frustrated!

Byte Me!

Computing for the Terminally Frustrated!

Robert P. Libbon

Illustrations by
Jack Ziegler

A BYRON PREISS VISUAL PUBLICATIONS, INC. BOOK

BOULEVARD BOOKS

NEW YORK

BYTE ME!

A Boulevard Book / published by arrangement with
Byron Preiss Visual Publications, Inc.

PRINTING HISTORY
Boulevard trade paperback edition / December 1996

Art by Jack Ziegler.
Cover design by Wendy Carlock.
Interior design by Kenneth Lo.
Editor: Dinah Dunn.
Assistant Editor: Heather Moehn.

The Putnam Berkley World Wide Web site address is
http://www.berkley.com/berkley

ISBN: 1-57297-204-1

BOULEVARD
Boulevard Books are published by The Berkley Publishing Group,
200 Madison Avenue, New York, New York 10016.
BOULEVARD and its logo
are trademarks belonging to Berkley Publishing Corporation.

PRINTED IN THE UNITED STATES OF AMERICA

10 9 8 7 6 5 4 3 2 1

Contents

DISCLAIMER.. ix

INTRODUCTION 1

CHAPTER 1: A CURSORY HISTORY OF THE COMPUTER... 7

CHAPTER 2: SELECTING YOUR COMPUTER........................ 13

    IBM or Macintosh?... 14
    What to Look for in a Computer 16
    Types of Computer Systems... 18
    Desktop: Home and Office 18
    Laptop: Your Own Digital Albatross........................... 21
    Notebook: Technology for the Indecisive.................... 22
    Palmtop: Executive Assistant 22
    Carrot Top: What a Pain in the Ass............................ 25

CHAPTER 3: PURCHASING YOUR COMPUTER 27

    How to Read a Computer Advertisement.................... 28
    Mail-Order Warehouse 29
    Retailer.. 32
    Fly-by-Night Electronic Storefronts Run by Pushy
        Importers 34
    Never, Ever, Ever, EVER Ask a Computer Jock to Purchase
        Your Computer 37

Contents

CHAPTER 4: SETTING UP YOUR COMPUTER 43

Unpacking and Breaking... 43

What You Will Need (Besides the Patience of Job, That Is)... 44

How to Set Up.. 46

Translating the Manual into English............................. 47

The Keyboard 52

The CPU: The Little House of Pain 53

The Monitor 54

The Cables.. 55

CHAPTER 5: PERIPHERALS.. 57

The Pointing Device.. 59

The Printer (Or How to Address an Envelope in 137 Easy
   Steps) 60

The Modem 63

The Scanner 64

The Speakers 66

Tape Back-up, Zip Drives, and Other Stuff You'll Never Even
   Consider Buying 66

CHAPTER 6: ACCESSORIES 69

Watch Out for Magic Stuff!.. 75

CHAPTER 7: ERGONOMICS.. 79

**CHAPTER 8: FIGURING OUT WHAT THE HECK TO DO
            WITH YOUR COMPUTER**............................... 83

The Software License... 83

Games 84

More Games 91

Parents' Games 92

Dull, Dull, Dull, Dull but Useful Software 92

Recent Software Trends 101
Shareware 102

CHAPTER 9: WHEN SOMETHING GOES WRONG 107

Getting in Touch with Technical Support 109
Getting Even with Technical Support........................... 111

CHAPTER 10: MULTIMEDIA 115

What Is Multimedia? 116
Big Deal... 117

CHAPTER 11: THE INFORMATION SUPERHIGHWAY 121

On-Line Services: Because You Can Never Have Too Much
    Artwork 125
Bulletin Boards: When Amber Monitors Are Too Showy 129
Internet Providers 129
The Internet 132
Internet Cafes: Where Communication and Cuisine Collide ... 155

CHAPTER 12: THE WORLD WIDE WEB 159

A Few Web Terms 161
The Browser.. 164
Forums on the Web.. 166
Mailing Lists 168
Security on the Web 169
Exploring the Web... 169
Using the Web... 175
I Have Seen the Future of the Web and It Looks Like Bad
    Public Access Television.. 185

CHAPTER 13: THE FUTURE 187

Ignorance Will Go Through the Roof............................. 187

Contents

There Will Be No Real-Time Electronic Conversation 188

Book Reports Will Be Really, Really Good 189

The San Francisco Giants Will Have a Disappointing
    Season 189

Disney Will Open Analog World 189

Patience? Forget It 190

This Country Will Go to Hell in a Handbasket 191

So What's the Conclusion? 191

AFTERWORD 195

APPENDIX A: THE FAQ (FREQUENTLY ASKED
    QUESTIONS) FOR THIS BOOK 197

APPENDIX B: COMPUTING COMPLAINTS 201

APPENDIX C: MUSIC CREDITS 205

GLOSSARY 207

Disclaimer

Ever since the 1994 baseball players' strike, litigation—not baseball—has been America's national pastime. That means I have to include a legal disclaimer here, instead of the personal tribute to Hal Lanier I had originally planned. Here goes:

This book is a parody of the popular For Dummies® computer book series and computing as we know it today. Anyone who would actually take instruction, advice, or guidance from a book entitled *Byte Me!* has no business attempting to cross the street, let alone filing suit against the book's publisher, its editor, or especially its author. Although this book is based on fact, so was the movie *JFK*—the point being that blind trust in a persuasively packaged, legitimate-looking product is not such a good idea (as borne out by Joe McCarthy, Michael Medved, and Snackwells). You, Dear Reader, will be responsible if you decide to follow any of the suggestions put forward in this book.

To be completely clear: DO NOT use this book as any sort of computing advisor. DO NOT believe everything you hear. DO NOT jump off a bridge, even if all your friends do. As for wooden nickels—go ahead, take 'em.

Byte Me!

Computing for the
Terminally Frustrated!

Introduction

Relax. I know how you feel. Every day, some tech-happy video journalist files another report from another convention in Las Vegas, trumpeting the latest in computer wizardry—and you still can't figure out how to turn off the speaker on your internal modem. Try as you might, the gap between you and the front lines of the Information Revolution seems to get larger with each passing hour. Unwarranted assumptions about your computer literacy are now being made by manufacturers, retailers, and technicians—for instance, that by now everyone knows the difference between single- and double-clicking a mouse, or understands terms like Plug and Play (which, by all rights, really ought to be called Plug 'n' Play), or is comfortable with standard file extensions like .BMP, .TXT, and .BAT. What the boys at Cyberspace Headquarters don't get is that the vast majority of computer users aren't computer-literate, easygoing, eager celebrants of the microchip era. They are tentative, slightly embarrassed, easily frightened, highly suspicious consumers who share a vague suspicion that the world is out to make fools of them—a form of paranoia usually associated with adolescence.

And no wonder. If the world feels a lot like high school these days, it's no accident. The geeks behind the glorious and fearsome Information Revolution—the guys writing code, hyping multimedia, laying down the Infobahn, wiring the globe, digitizing "Gilligan's Island," and expanding the World Wide Web—*want* it to feel like high school. Why? Because this time around, the geeks are in charge, and *you're* out of it. And no matter how hard you try to catch up, no matter how much money you spend, you'll always be a step behind. Because that's the way they want it. Every day, geeks reduce more and more of our existence to some binary expression: On/Off, 1/0, Mac/IBM, Liberal/Conservative, Hootie/Blowfish, Mulder/Scully. But what it really boils down to is the one binary expression we all know and fear, the one we've never quite gotten over: with it/out of it.

Fortunately, the geeks who have been on the Internet since it was a Defense Department freebie, the ones who use only lowercase letters, are going to see their plans for global gloating go to ruin against that most wonderful of human endeavors: the free market. In the final analysis, what's going to determine the character of cyberspace isn't the guys who know the most about it, but the ones who spend the most to use it. That's you and me, buddy. Think about it: Who gets the most out of an automobile, you or the mechanic on the assembly line who knows how the manifold goes in? For whom is that ugly oval Ford dashboard designed? Who is the target audience for all those commercials? You, that's who. If you've got a buck in your hand and you're looking to spend it, then cyberspace will be yours. Eventually. All you have to do is hang in there.

If you can accept the fact that computers are here to stay, you have the right attitude—because there are no emigrés from the Digital Revolution, just victims and volunteers. So far, you've probably felt more like a victim, but that's all about to change. This handy little

book is all you need not just to survive this technological mael-
strom, but to prosper from it.

There are a few basic features of the Information Revolution that
you should always keep in mind, whether you're contemplating
buying a new computer, pleading with a stubborn piece of software
to do what it's supposed to, or trying to make sense of the latest
nonsensical Web terminology . . .

Nothing You See on Television Is True

Television has always presented a stunningly inaccurate picture
of—well, everything. But you know enough about cars to see that
"Knight Rider" was hokum. You're familiar enough with the law to
know that few of Sheriff Andy's arrests would have stood up in the
Mayberry Court of Appeals. And you've had enough experience
with greed to know that if Claudia Schiffer gave up that video exercise program she's selling, and started cramming stuffed shells
down her throat . . . she'd probably gain about three pounds.

But most people don't know enough about computers to spot the
inaccuracies. (Some people don't know enough about reason to
spot the inaccuracies in "Sightings," but that's another matter.) So
when puff pieces about virtual reality games began to appear, you
got excited because press releases announced that VR would be a
viable consumer product "within the near future." You didn't know
that, in this case, *near future* meant the same as *sometime after
you're dead.*

And if you think that news reports are somehow more reliable,
think again. Reporters don't have any better a grip on what's happening with computers than you do. Nor do they have the time or

3

inclination to properly study the latest technological breakthrough. What they *do* have is three days to get a filmed piece in about some gadget the producer read about in *Popular Mechanics.* Since most of the reporter's work goes into thinking up cute, pun-filled intro and exit lines, the research turns out to be reading the company's press release about the product.

Presence Is More Important Than Product

Perhaps you've been disturbed by the tremendous gap between the marvelous claims of new computer technology and the miserable performance you get at home with the products of that same technology. Maybe your powerful new operating system hates your old spreadsheet program. Perhaps the latest edition of your Web browser frequently decides to delete a couple of directories on your hard drive. As you watch the stocks of the companies who manufacture this stuff climb through the roof, you rail impotently against your inability to make anything perform properly.

Quiet down; it's not your fault. High-tech businesses are only doing what they must in order to survive: they've become high-speed, as well. They have to be able to react almost instantly to market opportunity; it doesn't do any good to produce a handy photoshop program if you're the sixth one to come along. For these businesses, the common technique has become a catechism: Get there first and establish a presence, *no matter how good your product.* Once you've become a name, then you can worry about fine-tuning whatever it is you're selling. This is why computer stuff never quite works as well as it's supposed to: the priority isn't being the best, but the first.

You're Never Going to Get It

Not completely, anyway. This is the most important thing to remember. You will always, to some extent, feel left behind by the Digital Revolution. There is simply too much going on, too many advancements in hardware and software, to keep up on all of it—or even the parts of it that interest you. How do you think Bert Loomhead of Manchester, England, felt during the Industrial Revolution? One day, he's sitting at home with Mrs. Loomhead, winding cotton into a skein; the next day all the cotton is being wound by machine at a new factory down the street. He couldn't keep up with developments, either. So don't worry if you feel bewildered by the Digital Revolution. The truth is that you understand cyberspace as well as anybody. In fact, you're running that place. Because what drives the Information Revolution—what pushes it forward, fuels it, makes possible all the advances in digital technology, multimedia, communications, and entertainment—is the same thing that powered the French Revolution, the Industrial Revolution, the Russian Revolution, and Branson, Missouri: Money. Your money.

Thanks for buying the book.

Chapter 1

A Cursory History of the Computer

The history of the computer can be seen as a series of remarkable events followed by periods of analysis and adjustment.
Then again, the history of your hair can be seen in the same way. For any meaningful analysis of the computer, we're going to have to take a look at the momentous events that shaped the development of this remarkable tool.

600 B.C.   Greek mathematician Gaicus adds 2 and 2 and gets 4.

598 B.C.   Greek philosopher Jacchus adds 2 and 2 and gets 5. The ensuing argument lasts three centuries, spawning two major schools of Western thought: the followers of Gaicus, known eventually as the "Geeks," and those of Jacchus, known as the "Jocks."

243 B.C.   A trader from the East appears with a device that promises to settle the dispute: a rectangular frame in which parallel rods are set at regular intervals, with beads threaded onto the rods. By manipulating the beads up and down on the rods, precise mathematical functions can be performed. The device is called an abacus. Descendants and disciples of Gaicus and Jacchus meet to settle the matter, but are unable to make the abacus perform properly.

241 B.C. The trader from the East returns and explains that, in order to function properly, the abacus has to be tilted back or laid flat, so that the beads don't keep sliding down. The opposing groups quickly reconvene and perform the arithmetic. When the abacus reveals the correct answer to be 4, Jacchus's disciples immediately proclaim reality to be subjective, and wander off in a funk. Gaicus's disciples celebrate, and set about writing the first abacus manual.

A.D. 1642 Blaise Pascal builds the adding machine. This contribution to computing will be recognized in the twentieth century, when his name is given to a programming language that proves immensely popular. Pascal will lose its popularity only with the advent of C, a programming language named after the grade most programmers receive in high school English.

A.D. 1831 English mathematician and inventor Charles Babbage begins work on his Difference Engine, a machine capable of performing calculations accurate to thirty-one places. It is so complex, and its technical demands so far ahead of the time, that only in 1991 will a team of English scientists be able to actually construct a working model of Babbage's invention. Turning an unwieldy crank a few hundred times, the hardy team of scientists performs the Difference Engine's first calculation: $2 + 2 = 5$. Descendants of Jacchus's disciples suddenly reappear—but when the scientists realize their mistake and correct it, this time getting the right answer, the Jocks stomp off.

A.D. 1923 Analog computing reaches its zenith with the construction of an eighty-foot slide rule. Prominent thinkers turn their attention to the question of digital computing.

A.D. 1934 British mathematician Alan Turing—who will become the driving force behind Britain's cracking of the Nazi's Enigma code during World War II—coins the term "Artificial Intelligence" after seeing Buddy Ebsen in the movie *Banjo on My Knee*.

A.D. 1946 Bickering scientists at the University of Pennsylvania manage to come up with ENIAC, a vacuum tube computer so durable and predictable that it is named after durable and predictable English actor Michael Caine (reversing the letters in his last name).

A.D. 1948 The semiconductive properties of silicon are utilized in the transistor, which replaces bulky vacuum tubes. Ironically, silicon is also utilized in rubbery compounds known as silicones, which are used to create bulky vacuums on the tube.

A.D. 1957 The movie *Desk Set* opens. Starring Katharine Hepburn and Spencer Tracy, it details the tribulations of a research department undergoing computerization. At the movie's end, the computer overheats, smokes, and blows up. Starstruck electronics engineers begin designing machines that will overheat, smoke, and blow up after two hours; their efforts will come to fruition in 1966 with the invention of Jiffy-Pop popcorn.

A.D. 1975 A $400 Altair computer kit, marketed to hobbyists through a magazine ad, becomes the most popular mail-order item since X-ray glasses. Responding to the surprising demand for home computing devices, other companies jump into the arena. Competition between the two top firms, Tandy Corporation and Ron's Novelties Inc., is fierce. Ron's Novelties finally loses the battle with an ill-advised marketing ploy: the demand that customers purchase a hand buzzer with every computer.

A.D. 1977 The Apple Computer Company releases the Apple II personal computer. The fact that the Apple II is shipped as a complete unit bewilders hobbyists across the country, who resent having to take the thing apart before assembling it.

A.D. 1981 Microsoft Corporation, formed by the two guys who programmed the Altair, releases MS-DOS, or Microsoft Disk Operating System. MS-DOS is already being used in IBM's popular PC, and Microsoft convinces other PC manufacturers to use MS-DOS as well. In one notable example of persuasion, when the CEO of Compaq refuses to license Microsoft's operating system, he awakens the next morning to find a bloody disk head in his bed. Soon all Compaq computers are running MS-DOS.

A.D. 1993 Intel Corporation introduces its Pentium microprocessing chip. However, excitement over the Pentium's release turns to scorn when it is discovered that some of the chips perform calculations incorrectly. Intel's management responds to the public outcry by offering to replace every defective Pentium chip with a hand buzzer.

A.D. 1996 World Chess Champion Garry Kasparov defeats Deep Blue, IBM's formidable chess-playing computer, 4 games to 2. To the dismay of millions, Deep Blue neither sings "A Bicycle Built for Two" nor whines "Error! Error! Does not compute!" when defeated. Deep Blue's programmers, however, do both. IBM renames its chess-playing wizard "Deep Six" when the machine, learning that Kasparov refuses to grant a rematch, overheats, smokes, and blows up.

These are but the highlights of a global phenomenon that is trans-
forming our way of life. Can we find a thread running through each
of these events—perhaps some sort of leitmotif illuminating the
complex relationship between the human race, this world, and the
tools we use to understand and master that world? Nope.

Chapter 2

Selecting Your Computer

It's a fearful time, isn't it? Everyone else seems to know exactly what he's doing, while you're not even sure how to spell Compaq. Now you know how your parents felt when television first came along.

IBM or Macintosh?

The differences between PCs and Macs are becoming less and less significant. Regardless, this decision will determine your friends, your career, your self-image, your future spouse, the success of your children, and the way history remembers you. And once you've made your decision, *you can never change your mind.*

Apple makes the Macintosh computer, which is already too cute for many people. The last time anybody got this cute with the apple thing was back in the late sixties, when the Beatles tried to build an entire record company around their own disintegrating group and something called Badfinger. But you have to hand it to a company that won't let anybody else play with their operating system: they've got guts . . . and a 15 percent market share. Still, Mac owners swear that their computers are the friendliest, fastest, best-looking, and most reliable machines around. It would be hard to argue with them, were it not for their infuriating "Apple righteousness," that unique blend of condescension, snobbishness, and disgust that every Mac user presents to the IBM aficionado. This attitude will make it hard for non-Mac users to feel bad when Apple eventually gets swallowed by a larger company like Tonka or Hoover.

Apple pioneered the concept of user-friendly, intuitive interface design. Their philosophy seemed to be that a comfortable interface would make the computer less an intimidating piece of machinery than an entertaining, easily mastered tool. Rather than type in a command like "delete file 200," Mac users could drag a file folder icon over to an onscreen garbage can, drop it in, and watch the garbage can bulge. Similarly, dragging a file to a fax application would cause the computer to launch the file's application, convert the file to fax format, launch the fax application, send the fax, close the file and fax applications, and sit there looking smug.

PCs, by contrast, were built on the IBM philosophy that:

- Work is repetitive, tedious, and boring
- Computers can do much of this work for us; ergo
- Computers should be repetitive, tedious, and boring

IBM, a pioneer of the personal computer (and now reduced to a prefix for the word *clone*), designed their PCs around MS-DOS, the operating system put out by Microsoft. DOS turned every PC into a miniature version of IBM: a rigidly structured environment of directories and operations, none of which really communicated with or trusted any other, all working toward a common end by going in different directions. DOS was no friendly, icon-driven interface; you had to prove you knew what you were doing to run a PC. You couldn't just click on an icon to get something going; you had to remember the exact name of a program's executable file, get to the right directory, and type it in. As for programs sharing data, forget it.

PCs survived only because Microsoft, in contrast to Apple, decided to license DOS to anyone who wanted to build a computer. It was a shrewd move—soon, *everybody* from IBM to Häagen-Dazs was making PCs. Systems running MS-DOS now make up the lion's share of personal computer sales. So diverse is the DOS market that today's three most popular name-brand models are manufactured by different companies: Dell's Bankbreaker, Packard Bell's Frustrato Mate Plus, and the Acer Crash King.

After a few years, even the folks at Microsoft got tired of looking at a DOS prompt and produced a user interface that would effectively mask their operating system, much as the Apple OS does. That icon-based interface was called Windows. Windows and Windows-compatible programs could now run simultaneously, share data, and crash together. It was a marvelous step, much hailed by PC

The Ten Stages of Personal Computing

1. Ignorance
2. Fear
3. Excitement
4. Confusion
5. Wonder

6. Impatience
7. Frustration
8. Hate
9. Resignation
10. Lunch

users, and much derided by Apple users who didn't quite get all the fuss. Before long, Microsoft made sure that only the most intrepid (or the most errant) computer owner would ever run into that arcane set of symbols, "C:\". Today, Windows still includes the option to "Go to DOS," but being yanked from Windows' soothing blue sky to an inky screen with nothing but a cold, unforgiving C:\ feels less like "Going to DOS" than "Going to Hell." In fact, demographic studies have shown that of all the computer owners who ever clicked "Go to DOS," *at least* 99 percent of them immediately followed it up with this panicked input: E-X-I-T ⟨ENTER⟩.

Nowadays the qualitative difference between Apple computers and PCs is about the same as that between Coke and Pepsi. Once in a while, you really feel like one or the other, but on the whole you'll take whatever's cold.

What to Look for in a Computer

No matter where you look for a new system, you're going to find a baffling list of choices when it comes to system specifications. (This is one argument for purchasing by mail—you avoid that awkward moment when your salesperson realizes you know nothing about computers and starts dreaming of his name on the "Employee of the Month" plaque.) How much RAM? How large an internal cache? What size monitor? What kind of video card? How big a hard drive? What speed CD-ROM drive? What about a printer? You have to have a modem, right? It's pretty scary—the only question you're prepared for is "What color do I want?" and there isn't a whole lot to choose from there.

Good news: it doesn't much matter what you end up with. Whether you buy a top-of-the-line multimedia model or a stripped-down number cruncher, you're going to hate it within a week, so why worry?

There are a couple of reasons for this. The first, and most widely recognized, reason is that "state-of-the-art" changes every week. You know that old joke: What's the difference between a good haircut and a bad haircut? Two weeks. The same thing goes for a computer bargain and a computer rip-off. You'll love the deal you got only until someone else you know buys one, so give up thinking you have to find the computer love of your life.

But the real reason you're going to hate your computer is this: it does absolutely nothing to correct all the things that are wrong in your life. No matter how much you've tried to shut your ears to the hype that surrounds personal computing, some of it has leaked in. Some part of you really believes that just owning a computer will somehow make your life better than it is. Well, it won't. You might be able to balance your checkbook, but there won't be any more money in your account. You might have access to thousands of electronic newspapers, but that won't change the fact that the crosswords in the *New York Times* stink since Eugene Maleska died. And you might be able to amass a group of global pen pals, but you'll learn soon enough that people in Guatemala tire of you just as quickly as your next-door neighbor did.

So stop worrying about getting exactly all the right system specs. No one can actually see the system specs anyway, so you can always lie about them. You're going to lie about the price anyway, so why stop there? Tell everyone you know you just bought a Cray. Just don't tell them it's a laptop.

Types of Computer Systems

What kind of system you own—desktop, laptop, notebook, or palmtop—says quite a bit about how you see yourself. Do you like to think of yourself as an efficient mastermind? You'd be best off with a desktop. Perhaps you picture yourself as a mobile yet resourceful operative. A laptop might better suit your needs. Or maybe you just have a hot cup of coffee and you're looking for a coaster. Think palmtop.

Desktop: Home and Office

The desktop computer is fast overtaking the Christmas tree as the most dangerous electrical system in the home. This type of unit accounts for the bulk of computer sales, as well as for the bulk of mankind's frustration with computing. In fact, desktop is a misnomer, because it implies that your computing unit will find a happy home on top of your desk—implying, in turn, that there will be some desk left over after your computer is sitting on it. Wrong. You should stop thinking of this as a desktop and start thinking of it as a room eater, because no matter how you try to limit the space your computer uses, binary sprawl is sure to set in. Whatever the

Do-It-Yourself!

One option that might strike your fancy is to assemble your own computer from individually purchased parts. After all, a state-of-the-art computer's parts are worth only about seventeen dollars, so why not buy the parts and assembly guide yourself and have a ball? There is a precedent for it—after all, this whole personal computing thing started with a hobbyist's kit, didn't it?

Here's what you should do: after ordering all the parts you need (a computer magazine can tell you what they are), go to an electronics store and pick up a soldering kit. Explain to the salesman what you'll be using it for and ignore the snickering. Take the kit home, clear off a table you won't be needing for a while and wait for your parts to arrive. When your order does arrive, carefully unpack and label each part, making sure to inspect each piece for any damage that occurred during packing or shipping. Once you have ascertained that all the necessary parts are present and in good order, you can begin.

Don't make the mistake of starting immediately, though. You wouldn't expect a major league pitcher to enter a big game without warming up, would you? (Yankee relievers aside, that is.) Well, you're going to need some practice, too. Get in the swing of things by first assembling something that isn't nearly as complex, or as delicate, as the computer you'll be putting together. Something like a nuclear reactor.

Who are you trying to kid? You can't possibly put together your own computer! If you really feel like making something, put a hole in a pile of clay, add a little baking soda, and then pour a little vinegar on top. Presto! You've got yourself a little volcano! But leave computer assembly to those who are trained for it: underage Taiwanese kids and elderly Korean women.

room with your desktop was once called—study, rec room, garage—it will now and forever be known as the Computer Room.

The sooner you recognize the inevitability of your desktop's territorial lust, the better off you'll be. Look at it this way: you're not losing a room, you're gaining the bridge of the *Enterprise*. Whether you like it or not, you're going to be spending a whole lot of time looking at this thing, so make it a comfortable place to be.

Go out and buy one of those ergonomic chairs—the kind with no back. These chairs make great footstools. Then get yourself a fifteen hundred dollar ersatz-leather, adjustable height, tilt, armrest-angle chair. Make sure it also reclines, so you can kick back during those long, lonely spells between Web pages.

Get yourself one of those specially made mail-order computer hutches. You'll be amazed at how durable wood-grain contact paper over cheap particle board can be. Don't worry that your setup doesn't look as good as the one in the catalogue. This is just because the setup in the catalogue has no cables. Your system would only look that good if it had no cables, something that might impair your computing ability. Then again, it might not.

Put a lock on the door. If you live with someone, explain that the lock is to keep your attention focused on your work, and shut out extraneous noise and interruption. Although this is true, the actual purpose of the lock is to prevent someone from scaring the bejee-zus out of you as you enter the Pit of Hellfire during those last, critical rounds of Sim Hell.

Pick up a few sheets of adhesive-colored dots, and use them to code the food you leave around the desktop area. Use green for "prepared within recent memory," blue for "probably still edible—check with dog," and red for "unable to place within major food group."

Laptop: Your Own Digital Albatross

All that computing power in one compact, lightweight, elegant . . . fragile, power-sucking, outrageously expensive, easily lost or stolen, accessory-ridden extra piece of carry-on luggage! Laptops squeeze all the computing power of desktop units into a unit that fits comfortably on a surface slightly bigger than an airline tray.

With a laptop, your computing life is no longer desk-bound or even home-bound. You're free to travel without fear that you've forgotten something, or that some urgent business will force you to return home. And if your business involves traveling, the laptop will be your constant companion. Together, the two of you will spend countless hours searching for free outlets in airport lounges, booting up and shutting down for smirking airport security staff, and racing to save files before the last of that three-hour, fifteen-pound battery runs down.

Notebook: Technology for the Indecisive

It's a computer! It's a daytimer! It's a calculator! It's a reminder! It's a paperweight.

Notebooks are the electronic equivalent of those odd restaurant dinner specials that result from bizarre kitchen accidents. Nobody invented the notebook, because a notebook is just a laptop with a lot of stuff missing. Its proponents claim that it belongs in every executive's briefcase, but where it really belongs is on the Island of Misfit Toys, next to Charlie-in-the-Box and that weird ostrich-riding cowboy.

"But it's light!" say notebook manufacturers. So is an empty cereal box.

Don't buy a notebook.

Palmtop: Executive Assistant

Palmtops are enjoying a brief vogue these days, if only because they remind baby boomers of the equipment Spock and Bones used to bring down to the planet surface with them—tricorders, life-form locaters, planetary mineral analyzers, and the like. In fact, real palmtops serve much the same function as their fictional "Star Trek" counterparts did: they log, sort, sift, organize, and spit out a

great deal of information that is of absolutely no use when it comes to avoiding the same fate as Geologist D'Amato.

The earliest palmtops were digital versions of datebooks, designed to store phone numbers and appointments, hold cute little spread-sheet and note files, and make calculations. The public went for these classy organizers in a big way, so more features were added: alarm buzzers that signaled dramatic pauses during classic stage performances and funeral eulogies; alternate function buttons with user-friendly markings like Ю and ℥; little Find-a-Route programs that supplied directions to anyone traveling from one Unocal 76 Truckstop to another.

Apple, with a reputation for innovation and an almost uncanny feel for consumer ease, decided it wanted to be like everyone else for once and just throw a product out on the market. To this end, they decided to produce their own palmtop—but with a difference. Apple's palmtop would rely not on someone's cruddy typing, but on his cruddy handwriting. This unit would be able to take a scribbled note, save it, and immediately fax it to someone in Yemen who might be able to understand it. Early brainstorming sessions in Apple's marketing department produced a name for the little dynamo: "Palm-O." This was duly jotted down on a prototype of the machine, which promptly read it as "Newton," and a legend was born.

Professional and public response to the Newton's initial release was unanimous: "This ain't ready yet!" The furor puzzled the folks at Apple, who failed to understand why they couldn't get away with something that had become standard procedure. But Apple is nothing if not responsive. After much frenzied research and development, Apple recently made several innovations for its latest version of this mighty mite: A carrying case that disguises the Newton as a Game Boy and a shock-proof case for those inevitable times when the Newton is angrily hurled against the nearest wall. Next year: the Chia Newton.

Another recent development in the palmtop field is the production of Retro Palmtops. These little units have next to no memory, can't handle standard spreadsheets or word processing files, and forget to carry the 1. In fact, they're good for one thing only, and that is dialing up the World Wide Web. They sell for a little under five hundred bucks, which is still two hundred times the price of their closest competitor, the Drinking Bird.

The most extreme version (to date) of palmtop minimalism is the little gadget that receives one specific range of satellite data, like stock prices or sports scores. For instance, Sony's Modell 6 contacts a dedicated satellite to let its user know instantly what city the Cleveland Browns play in.

Carrot Top: What a Pain in the Ass

He has nothing to do with computers, but I can't stand the guy. On the other hand, he has a lot of accessories, and he knows what to do with each of them. That's more than you can say.

Chapter 3

Purchasing Your Computer

You have three options when purchasing a PC: buying from a large factory warehouse like Gateway; buying from a large retailer like CompUSA; and buying from a fly-by-night electronics storefront run by pushy importers. Each of these options stinks. Whether you're a first-time buyer or a savvy veteran of electronic disappointment, you're in for a rough ride.

How to Read a Computer Advertisement

If you're going to order by mail, you might as well learn how to read the ads. Here's what some of those complicated terms mean.

17.5[1] Megahertz Multimedia Computer

—*InTel*[2] Pentium Turbo Chip with Zero Socket[3]

—14.4 bps Modem[4]

—31" Monitor Included!!!!!![5]

—4 MB RAM upgradeable to 32 MB[6]

—Supports Industry Standard Parts[7]

—Plug 'n' Play Sound Card[8]

—Includes over $1,000 Worth of Software![9]

—Pre-loaded with Access to On-Line Services!!![10]

—24-Hour Technical Support[11]

—Revolutionary Keyboard Design!!![12]

---

[1] *Do you know why the headline is so big? Because the decimal point between the 17 and the 5 is really, really small, that's why. This is a 17.5 Megahertz computer.*

[2] *Intel is the foremost manufacturer of chips. InTel isn't.*

[3] *That is to say, there's no socket.*

[4] *In this case, 14.4 bps means exactly what it says: 14.4 bits per second. With this modem, America Online's irritating "Please wait while we add new art" message is a thirty-day sentence.*

[5] *True—unfortunately, the actual viewing area is only 4".*

[6] *True again, but there is a slight hitch—you can either stay with the 4MB SIMM chip that is installed, or buy 32 1 MB SIMM chips to upgrade to 32MB. There's no in-between.*

[7] *Needless to say, this refers to the auto industry.*

[8] *In other words, speakers aren't included.*

[9] *Includes five bucks worth of software.*

[10] *Pre-loaded with other ways to waste money!*

[11] *You guessed it—your technical support expires after one day.*

[12] *It's a Dvorak.*

Mail-Order Warehouse

If you ever decide to buy from a mail-order house, the first thing you'll have to do is bring a small hand truck down to the magazine store and pick up one of those Computer Shopper magazines for a little over twenty-seven bucks. This may sound a bit extravagant, but these thirty-pound booklets have complete listings for every electronic purchase you can make in the fifty states—not to mention those hard-to-find deals in Guam, Shanghai, Taipei, and that bastion of digital know-how, Belize.

(Helpful Tip: Before making your purchase by mail, be sure to check your local criminal statutes concerning nonpayment of sales tax, interstate transport of contraband, and especially the penalties for conspiracy to commit industrial espionage.)

Forget the first fifty thousand or so pages of color advertisements; these are directed at the corporate purchasing agents who can afford to pay top dollar plus 50 percent for brand names like IBM, Apple, Compaq, or Grechsmann. The smart shopper knows that the true steals and deals are way in the back, in teeny ads with teeny type, where vision-impaired federal investigators have a hard time making out the difference between "money-back guarantee" and "mosey-back guarantee." Now start hunting! Just follow these few simple rules, and you'll find some truly unbelievable deals:

1. Never trust unbelievable deals.

2. Avoid vendors who advertise "Incredible Bait and Switch Deals!"

3. If it costs more to call the company than to buy the computer, forget it.

4. Be suspicious if, when you call to order a computer the operator blurts out: "Hey, guess what! My mother's maiden name is Schmidt! What's yours?"

5. Always get your deal in writing. English writing.

If you don't feel comfortable enough to deal with the lesser-known warehouses, there are three or four companies that have national reputations—much like the one Union Carbide has in Bhopal. These companies are usually based in the Midwest, and for a very good reason. An address in Nebraska or Kansas inspires images of huge, sprawling warehouses with

What a Deal I Got!

Don't be tempted by special discounted units that have been factory serviced. Although such ads always imply that the unit was returned because the customer decided he didn't like the color, or was transferred to Nepal, it's just as likely the unit was returned because it short-circuited the Eastern seaboard, killing seventeen. Avoid temptation when you see these factory-serviced ads by substituting the word *pacemaker* for *computer*, and see how good you think the deal is then.

thousands of forklifts hustling thousands of pallets onto waiting tractor trailers, while hundreds of Drew Carey look-a-likes run around making spot-checks to ensure the speedy delivery of quality products. An address in Nebraska or Kansas also ensures that 99 percent of the public will never have the chance to drop in and see what the operation *really* looks like: an eight-member Korean family, working twenty-three hours a day in the basement of their rented house on a homemade assembly line inspired by an episode of "I Love Lucy," while a 17-year-old kid from St. Louis alternates between taking phone orders, answering the technical support line, and making sure the Federal Espress pickup happens. (No, that's not a typo. Better start checking those labels more carefully.) For these kinds of places, quality control amounts to counting everybody's fingers at the end of the day.

Still, many people have managed to pry decent computers out of warehouse companies. It just takes a little know-how and patience. As long as you know exactly what you want, exactly how much you are willing to pay for it, and exactly how long you are willing to wait for it, ordering from a warehouse can be as easy and rewarding as playing chess with a hamster.

Retailer

More and more retail houses are springing up to deal with those purchasers who, extending the computer/automobile analogy, feel the need to test drive the unit before they buy. It makes good business sense for retailers to have a long row of demonstration computers set up, so that an educated consumer can make an informed choice based on present comfort and future need. Of course, since there's never anyone around to help operate any of the systems, a computer test drive amounts to little more than an hour spent trying to guess screen saver passwords.

Retail houses give you all the trappings of personal customer service with none of the actual service. Every time you walk into one of these hellish places, some poor schmuck is trying in vain to return the software he purchased two hours before, claiming never to have told the salesman that he owned a Kaypro. The aisles are almost impassable, with boxes and boxes of junky discount software spilling out onto the floor (junky discount software you bought a week ago at full price). The guy in front of you always walks too slowly, but you can't get by because the aisles are too narrow, and he invariably stops in front of the section you want to check out.

"But wait!" you say. At least here there are actual English-speaking, name-tag-wearing employees—real live people who can show us what's what, even if it does take three hours to get someone's attention. What could be wrong with that? What, indeed? Where does it say that a 17-year-old part-time clerk in a high-volume, high-turnover retail business *can't* give you good advice on a three thousand dollar purchase? While you may think you're getting straightforward answers to your inquiries, here's what the answers really mean:

- "This is the database program you want." *This is the database program we've overstocked.*

- "They're pretty much the same." *It's almost lunch time.*

- "Within a year, you're going to need this much RAM to run anything." *I smell commission.*

- "Personally, I'd go for the Packard Bell." *I hate you.*

- "This is the best kids' game around." *You're never too young to learn about automatic weapons.*

- "We might have one downstairs." *I'm leaving and I'm not coming back.*

- "Okay, I think I've got just about everything you need: 386SX with 2MB RAM expandable to 4MB, a Hercules video card, 2400bps Hayes-incompatible modem, 21" amber monitor, Griswold 23 1/2 DPI dot matrix printer, and a keyboard with special numerical keypad pointing device." *Today's my last day.*

The alternative to getting help from a salesperson who is either dimwitted or malicious is to pick someone out of the crowd who looks reasonably intelligent, follow her around, listen to her conversations, and watch what she buys. I say *she* because, on average, women are better shoppers. Women aren't embarrassed to ask for assistance. Women don't hesitate to tell a clerk he's talking too fast, showing too little respect, or talking utter nonsense. Women don't mind bothering the manager. Most men, on the other hand, never willingly expose their ignorance to anyone, never question what a clerk says (for fear of being exposed as ignorant), and view calling the manager as an emasculating experience. Men should be careful when hovering near women shoppers, however—there are, after all, some emasculating experiences that are rather more painful than others.

Fly-by-Night Electronic Storefronts Run by Pushy Importers

Buying from these guys is indeed a bad idea. Even browsing at one of these operations is a bad idea. In fact, just reading the ads for one of these businesses can be dicey. You should regard electronics dealers—the kind that sell anything with a chip in it, from talking puppies to Scud missiles—the same way you regard three-card monte dealers. (If you don't yet know what's wrong with three-card monte dealers because you saw a guy actually win five hundred bucks and you'd know if he'd been a shill and he sure wasn't, *you're* okay. You're one of the few people smart enough to walk into one of these electronic storefront-type places and come away with a fantastic deal.)

Fly-by-night electronic discount stores rely on our own ignorance and greed to con us. We want to think that we could pick up a top-of-the-line computer for five hundred bucks, so we convince ourselves that there's a plausible reason to find such a bargain. The reason we come up with is this: *Hey, most of the stuff in this store is stolen! I've heard that for every shipment of electronic goods between the Far East and the United States, a certain percentage of the goods simply "disappears." Maybe this computer I'm looking at "disappeared" from its shipment and ended up in this shop.* That's *why the salesman says there's just the one. Wow, and he picked* me *to make this offer to! I can tell he likes me. Just for letting me in on this deal, I'm going to buy not just the computer, but one of those little plastic elephants, an ersatz Oriental carpet, a couple of adult videotapes, and some batteries made in Guam, too!*

You might not believe that people can do such a con job on themselves, but it's true—the continued existence of these perpetually "Going-Out-Of-Business" stores proves it. In order to safeguard yourself from the alluring offers made by these stores, here's a little key to understanding the true nature of electronic discount houses: everything you see and hear about them is the reverse of the truth. Remember this, and you'll be all right:

"Super electronic discount." *Low-rent junk rip-offs.*

"I go get you new one." *I go in back, cram cheaper model with similar name into box for what you think you're buying, apply plastic tape to make it look like it's the manufacturer's mistake, and offer to put it right into your trunk for you, you lame sucker.*

"I can make you better deal for cash." *Using a credit card makes this a federal crime.*

While purchasing from these dubious discounters is inadvisable, pretending to buy from them is a pleasant diversion. Walk into one of the stores when there are no other customers. The door chimes will alert the one salesman in sight, standing behind a glass counter crammed with calculators, watches, and cigarette lighters. As you enter he'll look at you with a combination of distrust, anger, and hope.

When he says "I help you?" reply: "Do you have any Pentium multi-media computer systems?" and watch the fun begin. A horde of salesmen will materialize and descend upon you like revelers at your surprise party, and drag you over to Suckers' Corner. There, they will show you the "absolutely best there is system," one so new "even NASA not have this one!" Ask if you can test drive the system, and then watch how many ways they come up with to avoid turning it on. One guy will be dispatched to the cellar to get the extension plug, whatever that is. He will never reappear, but every few minutes one of the remaining salesmen will wander over to the top of the stairs and scream something in another language. In the meantime, ask them how they can sell this system for only $4,400 if it's so good. Connections. Ask them if you can make a Griswold-Schmenken connection on the Internet with this unit. Naturally! Ask if the machine comes with the Kevin Mitnick Seal of Approval. But of course!

When you finally grow tired of yanking these fellows' chains, be careful how you go about extricating yourself from the store. You don't want to get these guys angry—there are fourteen of them that you can see, and who knows what's living downstairs in the basement. The easiest way to make a clean break is to whip out a cassette recorder, stick it in someone's face, and say "Alan Durham, Channel 3 Consumer Crimebuster. How much did you say this system costs?" while turning to face the storefront window. When you turn back, you'll be alone.

Never, Ever, Ever, EVER Ask a Computer Jock to Purchase Your Computer

At some point in your computer research, you're going to hit on this really lousy idea. You'll think: *Why am I trying to negotiate this morass of technological mire by myself, when there are experienced guides who can gracefully steer me to a safe digital haven?* (Okay, maybe this isn't exactly what you'll think.) Hey—the cable guy installed my cable, the phone guy put in my phone, and the ~~tooth guy~~ dentist fixed my teeth; shouldn't the computer guy put together my computer?

No. No, no, no, no, no, no, no. I hope this is clear. Please don't make the mistake of likening computer jocks to technicians. Computer jocks are not in the same category as people who perform rote tasks over and over again, like cable guys ("Where's the TV gonna be?"), phone guys ("Where do you want this?"), and ~~tooth guys~~ dentists ("Spit."). Computer jocks are more like investment advisors, theater critics, and children under six—people who believe the rest of the world should conform to their picture of reality. And just look how well these people have done: an imminent retirement meltdown, *Cats*, and Barney. Asking a computer jock to purchase your computer is like asking Wayne and Garth to pick out a bride for you—no matter what you want, no matter what you say, you're going to end up with Kim Basinger.

The first thing your CJ (computer jock) will do is ask what you want to do with your computer, and then he'll tell you you're wrong. He'll explain exactly how you're falling into the same trap as the rest of mankind by failing to take advantage of the full capabilities of technology. He'll talk about vast new vistas of human experience that will open up if you can find the courage to meet technology head on. He'll promise you a spot at the cutting edge of cyberspace. The entire conversation will take less than seven seconds, but by the time it's over, you'll have given your CJ carte blanche in fulfilling a lifelong dream: your own little KAOS headquarters.

Three months later, to your horror, you'll discover that what you've gotten is a lifelong dream, all right—except it's your CJ's idea of a lifelong dream, not yours: a completely subsidized Monster System of his own. Oh, you'll own the computer, and it will do everything you wanted it to do; but your stuff will actually constitute about 13 percent of the machine's total capability. The other 87 percent will be stuff that your CJ thinks is cool, wants to test, or has invented on his own, including:

- an operating system you've never heard of;
- something called *Windoes 2001*, which the CJ says is "way better than that Microsoft crap";
- a telephone line that mysteriously runs out of the building;
- a printer that uses ideograms for its default character set;
- a manual consisting of a xeroxed spec sheet for something called a "XYXONX," with "XYXONX" crossed out and "Your Computer" written above it;
- handwritten receipts for three-hundred-dollar parts;
- a CPU cover that looks suspiciously like three pieces of cardboard taped together (the CJ calls it a "green cover");
- a C drive, its volume named D1003–FJ, with 125 megabytes of your stuff on it;
- a passworded D drive, its volume named SHREDGUTS, with 850 megabytes of your CJ's stuff on it.

And it won't end there. Every time your CJ comes across something he'd rather not try out on his own machine, he'll drop by to demo the latest software for you—like an application that, with an ingenious combination of gum wrappers, paper clips, and used AAA batteries, circumvents the MS-DOS 640KB memory ceiling by assigning routine computer functions to your air conditioner. And forget about reporting minor problems—just mention that your trackball sticks a bit, and before you know it he'll have you fixed right up with a brand-spanking-new three-button wireless ergonomic mouse that works perfectly "so long as you don't double-click while there's an airplane flying overhead."

Very few people ever actually manage to disentangle their lives from that of their computer jocks; the lucky few who do get away find themselves left with a hostile machine, no money, inexplicable overruns on utility bills, and a computer room that will forever reek of curry. So make the journey into cyberspace alone, or with another innocent to keep you company. Computer jocks are best left to professionals.

Don't Upgrade Your Computer—
Downgrade It

It usually costs half the price of a better system just to upgrade your RAM, so there's really no need to try to improve your system, unless you just want to paint it. Rather than upgrade your present system, downgrade it. You'll find that the various components of your present system can serve nondigital functions about the house:

- A mouse makes an excellent Xmas tree ornament.
- Your old keyboard becomes a new waffle maker.
- That blank old monitor is also a sturdy picture frame.
- CD-ROMs, of course, make great coasters.
- That dull mouse pad is a wonderful mat for your cat's litter box.

Chapter 4

Setting Up Your Computer

Don't kid yourself—you're not about to take the time to carefully unpack, read through the manuals, fill out the registration cards, and observe all those picky safety instructions. You're going to rip that sucker open, haul out the CPU, plug in everything that looks familiar, and flip the main power switch, aren't you? This is what Plug and Play really means.

Unpacking and Breaking

Never attempt to unpack your computer alone. Computer components are carefully packed at the factory in brittle styrofoam, enclosed in easily torn plastic bags, and then crammed into cardboard boxes. Freeing them from these boxes involves hoisting the whole deal into the air, gripping the component through the silicon-sprayed plastic, and then pushing the carton toward the floor. There is no way for you alone to safely remove the CPU or monitor from their respective cartons without either dropping them, falling on your head, or hopping uncontrollably across the room until you encounter some sharp-edged piece of furniture. Play it safe and get someone to help. Hold on to the plastic-wrapped computer while your assistant yanks on the carton, and see who falls backward farthest when the computer pops out.

What You Will Need (Besides the Patience of Job, That Is)

1. A bunch of extra Phillips-head screws—they're sold in all computer accessory stores. You don't really want to have to chase down every screw that rolls off the table, do you? Especially since a lot of cute companies paint their screws black to make them look really hip—and almost impossible to find. Drop one of those little suckers on the floor, and you'll spend the next hour staring downward, until at last you discover the little guy—by impaling either

your palm or your kneecap. (Important note: missing screws always come to rest point up on the floor.)

2. One of those nifty computer tool sets with a snappy zip-up leather pouch. Don't worry that you don't recognize most of the tools inside—the only one you're ever going to use is the screwdriver, anyway.

3. One of the following: a) fourteen 30-amp outlets on separate breakers, or b) a plug strip plugged into another plug strip plugged into the extension cord running from the kitchen outlet where the toaster is plugged in.

4. A phone line with a reliable long-distance company (preferably with discount rates to Redmond, Washington; Portland, Oregon; and Orem, Utah).

How to Set Up

The most important thing to remember when setting up is this: you will be messing around with the back of this thing for the next month. No matter how careful you are when plugging in all the cables, phone lines, keyboard and pointer cables, power cords, and speakers, as soon as you push the computer all the way to the wall, dress the cables nicely, and clean up, you're going to need to take the unit apart.

Your very first setup should be done not on the floor, not on the kitchen table, and not on your computer desk but on a flat surface at eye level. While this makes for erratic typing, more importantly,

About That "Turbo" Button

Many machines have a "Turbo" button that allows the computer to run much better and faster than normal. Should you ever want your computer to run much faster and better than normal, push this button. If you're an idiot, don't push it.

it means that you don't have to bend in half to get a good look at the back of your computer. Since most of your first month's use will involve things like trying to tell the difference between the keyboard plug and the mouse plug, it's better that you don't have to contort yourself—especially since the little icons that label the two plugs are not only tiny, but the same color as the rest of the computer.

Translating the Manual into English

Your manual contains every essential fact about your new computer, as well as every nonessential fact about your computer. In case you're wondering, nonessential facts outnumber essential facts by a ratio of 1,000 to 1.

Like it or not, you're going to have to open the thing up and actually read some of it. Maybe not today, maybe not tomorrow, but soon. And you will find it difficult slogging, so here's a way to make it less tiresome: Read it aloud. Read it aloud in a mock villainous accent, as if you were some nefarious Chinese mastermind explaining gleefully just how you intend to enslave the world's population.

It's not half-bad that way, and it makes even more sense than *The Net*.

The first thing to notice about a manual is that the first thirty pages are taken up with dire warnings, like "Never defeat the purpose of the three-prong grounding-type plug," "Never use this product near water," and "Never attempt to service this equipment yourself." It all seems a bit overwhelming—but all the copyright notices, disclaimers, and safety instructions can be summed up in one simple, easy-to-remember statement: *Never actually turn this thing on.*

If you're lucky, the next portion of your manual will be taken up by a lovely greeting from the technical writers, who demonstrate their complete (and recent) command of the English language with the following:

> Congratulations on your purchasing the Engram M-5 486 Computer System! And welcoming you now to the great family of M-5 users from. We hope you.
> —your Manual Laborers

After this cheery message, the manual proper begins.

Table of Contents

This is your first indication that something is amiss. No page numbers are given, just sections and section subdivisions. This isn't done just to be different. This is done for a specific reason: when your computer manufacturer realizes the manual doesn't say anything about not touching that little exposed wire on the motherboard, they can easily, quickly, inexpensively, secretly insert a page in future manuals. That way, after you receive a shock strong enough to melt your ear wax, the manufacturer can claim your page with the warning must have simply fallen out—see, all the other manuals have them!

System Layout

After a very brief, very elementary description of the unit that nevertheless sails over your head, the manual embarks on a tour of the physical system, beginning with a nice schematic of the CPU interior. Every schematic of every computer has one thing in common: nowhere is there any indication of where the front of the machine is. Why not? Two reasons:

1. The guys who built the thing don't know until the last minute where the front is going to be.

2. You guessed it—in order to find the front, you have to take the cover off the computer, giving the dog another shot at drooling all over the motherboard.

Installing Memory

This is the only section anyone really ever reads, because everyone wants more memory than he has. Here is where you discover that your motherboard has four SIMM sockets (SIMM stands for Single In-line Memory Module, the memory chips you install to increase your RAM); that the first one is Socket 0 and looks nothing like Sockets 1-3; that your hands are six times too big to maneuver a SIMM chip into its socket; and that while you were reading the manual the dog drooled all over the motherboard.

The section also lays out in chart form the various possible memory configurations. Don't worry if your eyes glaze over as you try to identify the combination you want; it happens to everyone.

Common Problems and Their Solutions

Your heart leaps when you see this heading—not only do you understand every word in the title, but it promises help for the kind of problems that happen to ordinary folk like you and me. Do yourself a favor and don't bother. No matter how common your problem is, it's not in here. You might know three hundred people who have experienced the same problem—it's not in here. Why is this?

It's easy: manuals come with the computer, right? Now, if manuals have to be written before the computer is ever sold, how does anyone come up with common problems? (Some of you might be thinking: *They test them, that's how.* This reasoning shows a complete ignorance not only of computers, but of the entire capitalist system. Get real.) Common problems are those that the computer builders *think* you should have, and of course your idea of common and the manufacturer's idea of common might differ.

Here's a random sampling of common problems and their solutions, taken from the owner's manual for the Grechsmann Series-222 Pentium 133 Computer:

Error Message	Solution
Pointing Device Error	Contact dealer.
Bad CMOS battery	Contact dealer.
Evil CMOS battery	Contact dealer.
RAM BIOS error	Contact dealer.
I/O Parity Conflict	Contact dealer.
E/I E/I O Conflict	Contact dealer.

You didn't really expect the manufacturer to list "Contact *manufacturer*" as a solution, did you?

VGA Utilities

Almost half the manual concerns pre-loaded VGA utilities and display drivers. Just pretend this material doesn't exist. Understanding it is about as much fun, and as useful, as knowing exactly what your spleen does.

The Keyboard

Keyboards are torturous devices, good for little more than collecting little pieces of food you eat while typing. For a while there, it looked as though the keyboard was going to be the sluggard of the computer industry—a part that served its function well, looked and felt familiar to consumers, and hardly ever wore out. This, of course, was unacceptable, so for years technicians worked to make the computer keyboard fragile, weird-looking, and packed with redundancies. Finally, this past year the first wacky keyboards made their appearance. Improvements included a bulky wrist inhibitor at the front for ergonomic comfort and typing distress, as well as embedded multimedia speakers that serve mainly as beverage collection sluices. More and more features are being added to the keyboard to make it flashier, less modular, and much more prone to disaster. As a result, keyboard sales have tripled, a nice feat that will nevertheless be eclipsed by next year's model: a multimedia keyboard equipped with its own scanner. With this latest version, a keyboard malfunction—once an extremely unlikely $80 irritation—will have become a commonplace $300 computing catastrophe.

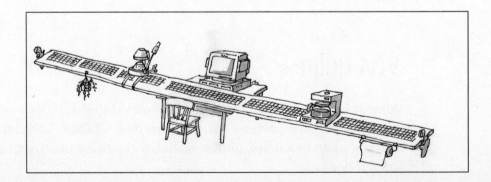

Typographical Errors That Would Have Been More Fun Than the Real Thing

1. MS-Worf for Windows
2. TurbotCad
3. Bork Nemesis
4. Under a Killing Moron

The CPU: The Little House of Pain

This tin box is the nerve center of your entire digital existence. (Technically, your CPU—or central processing unit—is part of your microprocessing chip, but many people use CPU to refer to the box that houses the chip.) Without this little guy, you'd sit at your keyboard just staring at the monitor (which, come to think of it, is what happens whenever you load a Web page). If you were to simply lift the screw shields, remove the thirty-seven Phillips-head screws, pry off the plastic retaining tabs, gently wrench the cover back until it clears its mooring tracks, and lift the lid, you would see the guts of your computer. Although it looks impressive at first, the CPU actually contains very little in the way of valuable stuff (much like the human body):

- 82 percent solder
- 13 percent plastic
- 2 percent wire
- 1 percent metal
- 1 percent silicon
- 1 percent dilithium crystal

Nestled amongst all the complex miniature circuitry are the CPU's essential components. Like the engine of an automobile, the CPU has many parts—including the motherboard, fan, hard drive, floppy drive, ribbon, bus, microprocessor, co-processor, power supply, and disk controller. And like the engine of an automobile, the fan is the only part you really understand. This shouldn't bother you, because you shouldn't ever think about messing with any of the other parts. Setting jumper switches, installing new chips and co-processors, and configuring odd drives is best left to a team of miniaturized scientists operating in a tiny, tiny submarine specially designed to maneuver around the CPU without destroying anything. The rule to remember (it's the same one you've been hearing since you were three) is this: If it's important, keep your hands off. And it's pretty easy to tell if something inside a CPU is important—it is clearly labeled as such, in microscopic letters indistinguishable to the human eye.

The Monitor

Technically speaking, computer monitors fall into two basic categories: 1) included, and 2) sold separately. Whichever monitor you end up with will have many adjustable features like contrast, brightness, horizontal alignment, vertical alignment, stretch, and degauss. None of them is of any use whatsoever. Studies have shown that the average user spends just over seventy minutes attempting to adjust these features, with a net display change of zero. Turn it on and leave it alone.

The Cables

Computers and computer equipment always come with removable power cables. This is so you won't have to go through the same ordeal you did when you had to replace the power cord to your television set. Oh, you never had to replace the power cord to your television? Well—on your VCR then. You never had to replace that power cord either? How about your stereo? How about your clock radio? You've *never* had to replace a power cord? What an uneventful life you must lead.

Okay, here's the truth: power cables are never connected to the things they're supposed to power so that you will lose one or two and be forced to buy some more. Fortunately, there is an industry standard for cables to make it easier to buy the right replacement. Unfortunately, that standard is for the rigging industry. The computer industry's cable standard, RS-232, is disregarded by just about everyone.

Chapter 5

Peripherals

The word *peripheral* was once an adjective, but it has been nouned. Peripheral now means "external." The following external devices are crucial to your computer productivity. Still, you will spend less time selecting them than you will picking out a new mouse pad. It's ironic that all these external devices were designed with but one object in mind: to have you open up the back of your computer and ruin everything inside.

Why would you have to open up your computer to use an external device? Because of the expansion card, the adapter that when plugged into one of the expansion slots on your motherboard's bus gives you a place to plug in your lovely new peripheral device. These days, when most systems come with modems, sound cards, and ~~mouses mice~~ pointing devices pre-installed, it might be a good while before you ever encounter one. But encounter it you will. One day you're going to buy that snazzy-looking trackball or flashy handheld scanner and learn the dirty little secret of peripherals: behind every handsomely packaged trackball or hand scanner, lurking somewhere within its snappy display case is the expansion card. Wrapped and sealed in its own special antistatic material, it is both the most delicate inanimate item you will ever handle, and the first thing that falls out of the box.

Bad Idea

Sometime in the future, after you've dropped three or four screws onto the motherboard while trying to install an expansion board, the following thought will occur to you: *Hey, here's something! If I had a screwdriver with one of those neat magnetic tips, the screws would never drop off onto the motherboard!* This is not a really good idea. In fact it's a dumb thing to do. Remember that old children's game Paper, Scissors, Hard Drive, Magnet? Magnet beats hard drive every time. If you don't believe me, try lending a co-worker a magnetic screwdriver when he's opening up his computer sometime, and see how he thanks you.

If you think about it, everything about the installation of an expansion card is an invitation to disaster. It's hard enough just to know what to do first: Open up the computer to prepare it for the card, and leave it sitting around while you wrestle with the static-resistant, grease-resistant, open-resistant packaging. Or take out the card first—and leave *it* sitting around while you open up the CPU, thus exposing your expensive new peripheral to everything the warranty says it should never ever come into contact with: air, light, noise, and thought (to say nothing of an occasional exploratory lick from the dog).

And just how are you supposed to install the card? Easy! Simply push the thing in just hard enough to break it if you do it wrong. And how do you know if you've broken the thing? Only by finishing up the installation, putting your computer back together, plugging it in, and turning it on to test. That's when you get the message: *Unprecedented disk failure . . . idiot.*

You might be thinking: Can't I just skip all this peripheral stuff, anyway? No. Like you, many people make the mistake of believing that, once they've bought a computer, they're completely equipped for a productive life in cyberspace. This couldn't be more wrong. Buying a computer with the belief that you've satisfied all your computer needs is like buying a spud and calling it Mr. Potato Head. Just as Mr. Potato earns the surname "Head" only after he has a nose, ears, lips, eyes, glasses, and a bowler hat, your machine is only a computer once you've added a terrifying and expensive number of extras.

The Pointing Device

The pointing device can either make computing a joy, or it can cripple you. Let's face it—you can't type to save your life, so most of your communicating is going to be done with your pointing device. Make your choice count.

The Mouse

The most common pointing device is the mouse. Its popularity is due less to its technological benefits than to its remarkable versatility. Sure, it moves the cursor on your screen—but it's also very good for reenacting the fateful telegraph scene from *Gunga Din*. And recognizing the mouse's apparently unique ability to collect unwanted matter, waiters in fancy Italian restaurants have begun using the mouse as a post-prandial dust and crumb picker-upper.

The Trackball

A space-saving version of the mouse, the trackball has a stationary base with a top-mounted ball that is manipulated to move the cursor. Trackballs are useful during those endless waits when either an hourglass or clock is parked in the middle of your screen—you can whip the icon around in a circle as fast as possible, and see how long before you throw up.

The Little Pad You Push Your Finger Around On

This is strictly for people who are nostalgic about rolling up little Elmer's Glue balls on their desk in elementary school. The action is the same. To manipulate your cursor, you move a fingertip around on a rubber pad about the size of an inspection sticker. Product studies have shown that it will take six years of regular use for your finger to become completely numb, at which point you'll have to use one of your remaining good fingertips. This gives you a good quarter century before switching to your bad hand—plenty of time to acquire the necessary ambidexterity.

The Printer (Or How to Address an Envelope in 137 Easy Steps)

The printer is the toaster of the computer world: it gets real hot when it's working, it always takes a little longer than you want, and you're forever opening it up to remove little pieces of stuff that are stuck inside. The big break you get with a printer is you don't have to install an expansion card to use one, since computers come with printer ports already installed. You have three basic types of printers to choose from: laser, ink jet, and "Jesus, they still make those?"

Laser Printers

Laser printers give letter-perfect quality, which would be great if you could write letter-perfect letters, but let's face it—you have nothing to write that is important enough to warrant a laser printer.

Besides, laser printers have almost as many options to set as your computer, and for some reason the manual is three times as thick. Other reasons to pass on a laser printer:

1. You don't quite understand how the word *laser* figures into all of this, but vague memories of James Bond strapped to a table ("I expect you to die, Mr. Bond!") trouble you.

2. Laser printers are so efficient that they demand a level of professionalism that is beyond you. As a result, a disappointed laser printer will often throw a fit and print out fifty sheets of paper with one ASCII character per page.

Ink Jet Printers

Ink jet printers are perfect for the average user. Unlike the eerily silent laser printers, these amiable units make friendly clunks, grind gears, and occasionally leave pools of ink on top of your documents. They're much lighter than they should be, break down often enough to make you feel superior, and create documents that look as good as you write—which is to say, they look as though they've put some effort into the deal.

"Jesus, They Still Make Those?"

These days, you can get a pretty good dot matrix printer in a box of Crackerjack. Between you and me, you're better off with the little plastic magnifying glass.

Digital Homework Excuses

1. My server was down.

2. My hard drive crashed.

3. I thought this was a virtual test.

4. The dog ate my floppy.

The Modem

Modem stands for *mo*dulator-*dem*odulator. What that means no-body knows, but it sounds good. The modem is your computer's all-important link to the outside world. Through the modem, you can get online, surf the net, browse the Web, download the virus, pile up the message units, hang the computer, talk to the FBI, get entrapped by the FBI, stay in touch with people you never wanted to hear from again, play real-time games with people you'd sooner see dead, and generally watch the rest of the world fly by you.

There are currently one hundred and twenty-three trillion types of modem on the market. How do you know which one to buy? Just pick one. If you get a lemon, who cares? Because better modems are being turned out every other week, you'll be changing modems more often than you change underwear. There will be plenty of chances to try them all. The only real choice you have in the matter is between an external and an internal modem, and the difference there is just the price.

External modems cost more than internal modems, for two reasons: 1) external modems require expensive and tasteful plastic covers, and 2) using an external modem cuts into the supplier's profits, since it shortens the odds that you'll break the thing during installation and have to buy a new one.

Modems are rated by the speed at which they transmit data—bps, or bits per second, to be specific. Just a few years ago it was considered very high-tech to own even a 2,400 bps modem; today anything less than a 14,400 bps modem is considered useless, and even that will be too slow by the time this book appears.

The Scanner

Many people are curious about just what a scanner can do, and the answer is: yes, you can scan your ass.[1] You can also scan the xerox of your ass that you made on the copier at work. Once on your computer, you can even import the scanned picture of your ass into a paintbrush program and edit, copy, paste, dither, facet, pointillize, greyscale, rescale, push, file, index, brief, debrief, or number your ass. Then you can e-mail your friends a bitmap of your edited ass, and get a bunch of other people's asses over the Internet in return.

The rest of us will wait until you're finished.

Now that we've taken care of that, there's serious work to be done with a scanner. You can scan all of your old, yellowing school, wedding, honeymoon, vacation, and party photographs onto your hard drive, to keep as long as you like. It's a little harder, passing the monitor around the room instead of a scrap-

---

1. On a flatbed scanner, that is.

book, but it's well worth it for the clarity and durability of the pictures. An added benefit is that you can edit scanned images, just as you edited the picture of your ass. With a little practice, you can learn to digitally remove lampshades from your head, make it look as though Teri Hatcher or Jared Leto was your date for the junior prom, and obliterate any evidence that you ever wore mood rings or tube tops. This process is known as "Zeligating," since it involves the same process that made the movie *Zelig* possible. The process that made the movie *Toy Story* possible isn't yet available, because no one has yet figured out how to reverse the process that turned many of the film's actors into rendered characters. To this day, Tom Hanks is still stuck in digitized form, which explains his interest in the script for *Gumby: The Movie*.

The other thing you can do with a scanner is scan in important papers. But don't get rid of the originals—no one will accept scanned images because of the chance that they have been Zeligated.

You might think that once you have scanned your pictures your papers, and your ass, you have no further need for a scanner. Not true! Flatbed scanners are also great for pressing small pieces of clothing and warming up bagels.

The Speakers

The speakers you use for your multimedia system play a vital role in your computing enjoyment, so your reputable computer dealers always include a pair of speakers with a new multimedia system to get you started. Just unwrap them, plug them into the jack on your sound card, try to find yet one more free outlet, power them up, sit back, and listen! It sounds like crap! You can get the same sound from an open value-pack box of Rice Krispies. Why is this? If you haven't guessed by now, this is because the same company that supplies the crappy little speakers also makes good little speakers!

Tape Back-up, Zip Drives, and Other Stuff You'll Never Even Consider Buying

The last few pages of any computer catalog, magazine, or advertisement usually concern themselves with real hardware: hard drives, zip drives, tape drives, floppy drives, CD drives, network adapters, etc. You can tell this is serious stuff, because they don't sport names like Speedy or Putzo, like the rest of the crap you buy. This stuff carries names like T-180/AAX, or Ether NxNW, or 86-86AllSetBlue95-Blue95-HutHut. It's kind of like looking in the back pages of a Rite-Aid newspaper supplement for aspirin, and finding a few Magnetic Resonance Imagers for sale. Play it safe—stick with *The Lion King* mouse pads and you'll be fine.

Chapter 6

Accessories

It's amazing what they can do with velcro and plastic these days.

The Mouse Pad

The lunch box of the nineties. Gullibility and redundancy reach their zenith with the mouse pad, which, after all, is nothing more than a flat surface placed on a flat surface. The genius who came up with these is the same guy responsible for Nail-Outeners, those handy gadgets that you use to remove protruding nails—that is, if you failed to notice that your hammer came with its own nail-outener, opposite the head. (Please, no letters from you ball-peen losers. If you bought the wrong hammer, it's not my fault.)

The Anti-Static Wrist Strap

The most impressive accessory you can ever buy is the Static-Free Computer Repair and Installation Wrist Strap, which comes with a free package of NASA Astronaut Breakfast Bars (a nutritious space food made of particle board and carob). This is the strap that computer manuals recommend you put on whenever you come within three feet of your CPU.

A static discharge between you and your computer, like just about anything else you ever do, could result in a loss of data. By donning the strap, hooking up one alligator clip to a terminal on your car battery, and the other to the nearest source of neutrino emission, you safeguard your transactions against static discharge. (Alternatively, you can spray the whole unit with Cling-Free, and go on petting the cat as you work.)

The Disk Label

The accessory you can't live without is the Official Floppy Disk Label. Don't ever make the mistake of using something like an Ordinary Little Stick-On Label to mark your disks; it would be totally inappropriate to use something so pre-digital. No, make sure you always use the special Official Floppy Disk Label (the Official Label of the 2002 Winter Olympics), the one that fits the disk's label space with barely a millimeter of clearance on all sides. Once you master the art of applying these labels without having to tear them off and try again, you'll be glad you chose to use these Official Floppy Disk Labels. Why? Because these labels have Official Floppy Disk Label *Lines* on them, for efficient labeling. Accept no substitutes.

The Stupid Set of Little Keys

Many computers come equipped with a pair of little keys that resemble alarm keys. These are for locking the computer. How do they work? They prevent anyone from turning on or accessing your

computer when you're not around. They do not prevent anyone who is frustrated by your locked computer from kicking the CPU across the room.

Don't use these keys.

The Monitor Swivel Stand

Every monitor comes equipped with one of these, because you never know when you're going to need to swivel your monitor 11 degrees to the left or right. Note that I don't say up or down. Although the swivel stand does have vertical adjustability, trying to smoothly adjust the monitor up only results in shoving it off the stand completely, while trying to tilt it down pulls the plug out of the back of your CPU. Give yourself a break and just park the monitor on top of your CPU (unless you have a tower, of course) without the stand. Stick the stand underneath your CPU, which is where it really belongs. Now you'll be able to rotate your computer for easy access to the ports and plugs in back.

The Multimedia Microphone

How does a multimedia microphone differ from an ordinary microphone? By the length of the cord. Ordinary microphones, made for ordinary use, have six-foot cords. Multimedia microphones, made for Quasimodo's use, have three-foot cords. Why is this? Three words: multimedia extension cords.

Cable Hiders

Tired of that rat's nest of cables emanating from the back of your computer hutch? Buy some of these plastic cable hiders, and pack those messy cables away!

Cable Hider Hiders

Sick of that rat's nest of cable hiders emanating from the back of your computer hutch? Buy a few of these cable hider hiders, and cram those messy cable hiders away!

Cable Hider Hider Hiders

This is beginning to sound like *The Cat in the Hat*, isn't it?

Electromagnetic Field Scramblers

These handy devices neutralize the harmful electromagnetic fields produced when a bunch of electronic appliances—computers, monitors, scanners, etc.—are clustered together. Anyone concerned about a potential electromagnetic health hazard can do one of two things:

1. Contact a consulting firm that specializes in identifying electromagnetic fields. These companies test and define household electromagnetic fields with an eye toward eliminating the danger, and lease special "field scramblers" to break up the cumulative electromagnetic fields.

2. Stop watching "Unsolved Mysteries" and read up on the subject. Scientific studies to date have failed to produce a speck of evidence that electromagnetic fields are harmful. When these studies began to examine the effects of electromagnetic fields on the body, newspaper headlines and television features trumpeted the possible danger. Citizens' groups, unwilling to wait for the results, pressured utility companies to bury all new power lines. The value of real estate near substations plummeted. The panic gave rise to companies whose only mission is to test and define household electromagnetic fields with an eye toward eliminating the danger.

In the meantime, those boring, drawn-out scientific studies turned up no evidence of risk. Naturally, the press treated these glad tidings with the usual contempt it shows for information that is merely true, and not urgently terrifying. Not one tabloid news program aired a five-minute follow-up piece entitled "What You Can't See *Won't* Kill You." Newspapers buried the story while giving plenty of space to the latest potential disaster: a horrible flesh-eating bacteria.

The Deadly Virus

Much has been written about the computer virus—a self-propagating, insidious piece of code that can wreak havoc on the computers it infests. Transmitted through shareware, shared floppies, bulletin boards, the Internet, and even e-mail, computer viruses can cause anything from a minor disruption to a loss of critical data to a crash from which there is no recovery. If you suspect you might have a computer virus, watch for the following symptoms:

1. At least one program fails to perform as expected.
2. Your computer displays messages that you don't understand.
3. You can't find many of your files.
4. Game programs run too slowly.
5. Your friends' machines seem to run much better than yours.

One or more of the above symptoms means that a) you have a computer virus, or b) you have a computer. Frankly, most viruses do less damage to your computer than you do on any given day, so it's a waste of time to worry about them. Digital hypochondria is something we can all do without, since it would probably qualify under the Federal Disabilities Act. If you're truly concerned about viruses, try using a little common sense. Pretend that the computer is your stomach, and then act as though anything you put into it is food. Maybe then you'll think twice about taking that tasty piece of shareware from sHpLeCko@weeyurd.net.

If it makes you feel any better, go ahead and pick up an antivirus program. Don't be surprised, though, when it identifies eight different viruses the very first time you run it. Almost any antivirus program you buy will load a few viruses on your computer during installation, just so it can find them the first time you run the application. It makes you feel smart for having bought the thing.

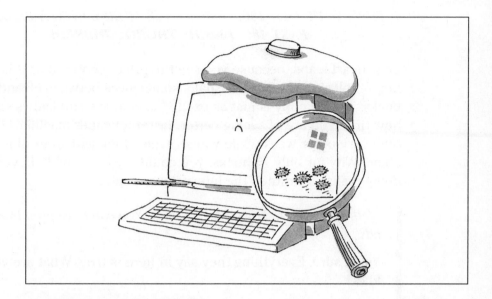

An Anti-Flesh Eating Bacteria Device—now *there's* an accessory worth the money.

Watch Out for Magic Stuff!

You're going to be constantly running into magic stuff. What is magic stuff? It's the product that costs one tenth of what everyone else is paying and does exactly the same thing! We've seen magic stuff come and go over the years: the special attachment that instantly transforms your black-and-white television into a color set; the little pill that quadruples your gas mileage; X-ray glasses. The difference these days is that computer technology is so far removed from human existence that we have a hard time recognizing magic stuff when it comes along. Say you're leafing through one of the seven thousand electronic catalogues you regularly receive because you actually registered your software. You turn the page, and a screaming headline catches your eye:

TURN YOUR OLD 286, 16MHz PACK HORSE INTO A BLAZING FAST 486, 100MHz THOROUGHBRED!

Your heart leaps, because you see the price (centered as it is in a huge explosion graphic)—usually somewhere between 60 and 100 bucks. The ad copy is just as excited as you are and knows exactly how tired you are of seeing better, faster, cheaper machines come out every other week while you struggle along with your old machine. Why for only 75 bucks, you could . . . get ripped off, you suddenly realize. And then the internal war begins.

–*Well, there has to be* something *in it. You can't just print fraudulent ads.*

–Yeah, sure. Everything they say in here is true. What are you, an idiot?

–*But if it's really bogus, why are they charging so much for it? If it's fake, you'd think they'd make it really cheap.*

–Hello, are you a complete moron? Wise up. Everyone else is buying the real thing.

–*Hold on a second. Have you ever considered this: Maybe all the stuff everyone else is buying is way overpriced, as part of a techno-conspiracy to keep prices artificially high. Maybe a computer only costs a buck and a half to build. And maybe—just maybe—this 286 to-486 converter thing is real, and its manufacturer is simply refusing to take part in this huge conspiracy by offering it at a fair price!*

–You've completely lost your mind.

–*Hey, isn't it worth 75 bucks to find out?*

–Haven't you forgotten something?

–*What?*

–You don't even own a 286.

–*I could buy one.*

The crazy thing about magic stuff is that you always have this reaction, no matter how many times you've looked at other magic stuff. The only way to be certain that you will never fall for magic stuff is to convince a friend of yours to buy some, and then watch him wise up.

Chapter 7

Ergonomics

Miriam Webster's dictionary (not to be confused with a Merriam-Webster dictionary) defines ergonomics as "the field of study concerned with selling oddly shaped objects for great sums of money." The geniuses behind ergonomics play this one brilliantly, seizing upon public gullibility when it comes to anything to do with computers. What else but gullibility could explain the success of the ergonomic chair, for crying out loud? Before computers came along, was there something fundamentally lacking in our understanding of sitting? Did we have to rethink the whole chair concept because we learned that people actually sat in the things? What if working with computers involved standing instead of sitting? Would we all be wearing Ergonomic Earth Shoes? Or would we be strapped into Ergonomic Slant Boards?

The essence of ergonomics is its reliance on counterintuitive design. People find it much easier to believe in things 180 degrees removed from their experience than in things that are only a little bit different. This is how we ended up with the following ergonomic innovations:

- Backless rolling seats that force users to half-kneel, half-sit in a position of constant supplication;

- Wrist-pads that make everyone type like Charles Nelson Reilly;

- Trackball and mouse pointers designed by Henry Moore with price tags to match.

The truth is, you can safely ignore ergonomics as a silly fad until it is generally accepted by the scientific community. You will know it has become accepted when they start manufacturing ergonomic guns.

Working Out?

A report by the President's Council on Fitness recently predicted that by the year 2010 (as opposed to the movie *2010),* 43 percent of all Americans will be spending 28 percent of their combined work/leisure time in front of computer screens. The council found this alarming, because 37 percent of all Americans already spend 17 percent of their leisure time watching television, and 22 percent of their work time watching the clock. The general upshot seems to be that fitness in the United States will decline drastically, as more people spend more time simply sitting. The council's report recommended that the following standards be implemented by computer manufacturers to help stave off this crisis:

1. The ball used in any mouse or trackball pointing device should weigh at least 30 pounds.
2. Depressing the 〈Enter〉 key should require two hands.
3. To exercise the neck, monitor stands should be equipped with hydraulic pistons that gradually raise and lower screens plus/minus 6 inches.
4. CD-ROM drives should rapidly eject compact disks in random directions, testing hand-eye coordination.
5. There should be a special tax deduction for users whose computers are powered by treadmills or bicycles.

Chapter 8

Figuring Out What the Heck to Do with Your Computer

Naturally, as soon as you have set up your computer you're going to want to do something neat with it. Unfortunately, you can't—for that, you need some software. It's true that all computers come with a bunch of software already installed on them, but that stuff is either practical and dull (printer drivers) or frivolous and dull (apes tossing a nuclear banana back and forth). Anything that looks good is just a demo of the real product, not a complete version. This package of useful dullness and frustrating entertainment is called "bundling." The moral here is: if you want to do something neat on your new computer, buy some software before the unit arrives.

The Software License

Although buying software seems a simple enough task, you should know that it is, in fact, a legal minefield. The software licensing agreement that comes with every purchase—the one thing most people feel comfortable giving to the cat, dog, or baby to play with—is a legally binding contract that carries more obligations than a favor from Don Corleone. Let's take a look at one, and actually read it this time:

IMPORTANT—READ CAREFULLY BEFORE OPENING SOFTWARE PACKAGE AND/OR USING SOFTWARE. By opening this package you indicate your acceptance of the following Software License Agreement, NAFTA, GATT, and the Designated Hitter Rule (AL only).

SOFTWARE LICENSE AGREEMENT
This Software License Agreement, including the Warranty and Special Conditions not included in this agreement but generally kept under lock and key in the utility closet at the Palm Desert Taco Bell, is an entirely legal agreement between you (henceforth, "you") and us (henceforth, "us"). By opening this package in order to get to this agreement you have in fact already agreed to all of the terms listed below.
1. GRANT OF LICENSE. This agreement entitles you to install this software on ONE computer ONE time, to make ONE backup copy of the software and mail it to us so that we may safeguard it for you. You may not install this software on another computer unless we (another way of saying "us") receive a notarized document from you stating that you have in fact deleted the original copy from the first computer, along with sworn depositions from two eyewitnesses to said deletion.
2. COPYRIGHT. Any rebroadcast or retransmission of this game is subject to review and/or approval by the National Football League (Paul Tagliabue, Commissioner), the Council of Elders (Elrond, Chairman), the League of Red-Headed Men (Jabez Wilson, Member Emeritus), and the coaches, trainers, and the rest of the 1967 World Champion Green Bay Packers (Jerry Kramer, Poet Laureate).
3. YOUR RIGHTS. Just kidding. You don't have any.
4. OTHER RESTRICTIONS. No right turn on red within NYC limits. Offer good except where no good.
5. ESSAY TEST. Write a coherent essay, no less than 500 and no more than 250 words, on one of the following topics: a) C+ is an Appropriate Name for that Programming Language; b) Adding "Smell" to Multimedia Is a Really Bad Idea; c) Why Not 33 Bits?

Games

Increased productivity might be the reason you have a computer at work, but what drives the computer industry isn't the tremendous potential for efficiency, but the enormous potential for wasting time. Companies might pay millions to increase efficiency, but employees will fork over trillions to get around it. Ask yourself which came first—the Boss Key or the Digitizing Tablet?

Rating Computer Games

Computer graphics have improved to the extent that they now rival Bugs Bunny cartoons in their depiction of violent action and sexual activity. (Admit it—that robot she-rabbit who entices Bugs into a high-voltage kiss is way sexier than Tia Carrere.) Responding to an implied threat of criticism, software producers announced that they would issue warning symbols with their games as a public service to concerned consumers. Their altruism was questioned, however, when the warnings were released:

☺	Nothing here that would excite anyone.
☹	Warning! A couple of things get broken. Someone screams.
!!	Warning! Contains revealing negligees and graphic gunshot wounds.
X	Warning! Bitchin' babes with torn togs making mincemeat of scabby skinheads.
⊛	Warning! What the men and women do in this game is too intense for you ... sissy.

Arcade Games

Arcade games are enormous fun. They're not just incredibly realistic, but once you've spent 200 quarters to buy the software, playing them is free! Anyone who has ever spent a week's allowance or paycheck pumping change into arcade machines loves these software marvels. One word of warning, however: the big difference between real arcade games and arcade software is what happens when you slam the machine in a fit of frustration.

Sports Games

Sports games employ the latest graphics technology to give you an exciting, in-your-face sports experience. Unlike crude, pre-digital sport-based games that involved holding player statistics cards, rolling dice, and moving pieces around on a board, today's computer games take all that arduous exercise out of the game. Superb sound, stunning visuals, and a range of complex options combine to give you that real game feel, while ensuring that the only time you'll have to move a muscle will be when you reach for the six-pack by your side. You get that "at the game" emotional high without ever having to actually play the game. In fact, you've never even gone to the game, because that would require you to get your sorry butt out of that sport-watching, computer-game-playing recliner.

Adventure Games

Adventure games used to be rather primitive, opening something like this:

You are in the dark.

Then you had to type in a command, like:

Turn on teh light.

The game would spit back:

''Teh?'' What are you talking about?

You'd correct yourself:

Turn on the light, you idiot.

And then:

''Idiot'' isn't here.

You'd write:

Oh yeah? I'm looking at him.

After a few more scintillating exchanges, you'd get the light on just in time to be eaten by some indescribable beast, at which point the game would ask if you want to start over. You wouldn't, unless you felt like typing in every vulgar word you knew just to see whether the game would recognize it.

Nowadays, you don't have to type in commands to manipulate objects; you can just use your pointing device. You don't have to imagine the dank dungeon in which you find yourself, or try to picture the foul beasties that threaten you with dripping claws and jagged molars—the games show you, in stunningly rendered graphics. Of course, the beasties are always less scary than you imagined when you couldn't see them, and the wizard you thought was so cool always ends up looking pretty doofy in that hat of his. What's more, several characters sound too much like rejects from "Masterpiece Theatre" for your taste. All in all, the experience is reminiscent of the first Lord of the Rings calendar you saw: a real nice try by some hard-working people, but really nothing like what you pictured.

Simulation Games

Concurrent with early text adventure games were war/flight/submarine/custody battle simulations, which gave players the wonderful opportunity of seeing what the world would be like if everything were made out of toothpicks. Toothpick F-14's swooped down on unsuspecting toothpick aircraft carriers, moored inconveniently in the waters surrounding toothpick Manhattan; toothpick tanks fired punctuation marks at faraway toothpick bunkers, with the ensuing explosions looking remarkably like flying toothpicks—and all to the incredible simulated static of the PC speaker.

These days the simulated Tomcats look, sound, and perform exactly like the real thing, as do the tanks, submarines, and other engines of destruction. Yet all the bells and whistles haven't changed the most satisfying part of a simulation game: selecting "Outside View" and watching yourself crash your F-14 onto the deck of a carrier.

A Word about Beta Testing

Beta testing is a phase of product development during which unpaid ordinary joes test new software and report problems to the manufacturer. For some reason, the dubiousness of this process escapes most people—no doubt because "You can be a beta tester" sounds a lot sexier than "You can be our guinea pig." Why should software companies get away with having you do their R&D for them? You don't see Black & Decker advertising for people to beta test their experimental chainsaws, or bungee cord manufacturers looking for "men and women interested in the exciting field of jump product research."

Board Games

One thing computers have done is eliminate the backbreaking labor involved in setting up and playing board games like Monopoly and chess. Multimedia versions of popular board games have introduced a whole new element to these family games: discomfort. Board games used to involve actually gathering around a table, setting up game pieces, and maneuvering them across the board. With computer board games, opponents no longer face off against one another; they sit side by side and argue about who gets to sit next to the mouse. More time is spent selecting which view of the game board to use than actually playing—somebody wants a direct overhead view, someone else refuses to use anything but an isometric view, and there's always one idiot who prefers the view that makes the pieces four stories high.

POV: You

One of gamedom's breakthroughs came with a bloody 3-D game called *Wolfenstein*. The basic idea was simple: a straight shoot-'em-up from the point of view of the player. The game had several goals:

- Kill everything that moves, as horrendously as possible
- Pick up treasure
- Massacre every living thing in sight
- Explore every room, level, and secret passage
- Kill, kill, kill
- Go back and kill some more
- Start over and see if everything can be killed a little more horrifically

The first version of *Wolfenstein* was released as shareware, a tactic glommed directly from crack dealers who hand out free samples of their goods. It worked; *Wolfenstein* took off. *Spear of Destiny* followed, as did a lame outer space version called *Blake Stone* . . . and then came *Doom*.

Doom put the player in a post-nuclear acid-bathed alien-invaded Disneyworld, and peopled the scene with mutants almost as scary as the real inhabitants of Disneyworld. *Wolfenstein*'s robo-killer looked like Regis Philbin when compared with *Doom*'s horrible cast of characters: fireball-hurling apes; great skull-spitting floating Ned Beatty heads; machine-gun-toting members of Right Said Fred; invisible Sean Penn–types that batter you while muttering incomprehensible curses; big boiled hams with legs; screaming mutant Orel Hershisers; and, of course, Roddy McDowall.

The makers of *Doom* shrewdly realized that, sooner or later, they'd run out of neat critters for players to kill—so they encouraged the development of shareware programs with which players could make their own *Doom* levels, scenarios, and villains.

Doom retained its popularity while spawning two successors, *Heretic* and *Hexen*, which added fun features without detracting from the game's essential entertainment concept: nauseating carnage.

More Games

MYST changed everything. This ground-breaking "game experience" proved that a successful multimedia game didn't need a third-tier Hollywood celebrity speaking five-second snippets of inspired dialogue, like "Hmmm . . . we have failed to defeat the Imperial Cleghornes! Perhaps you should spend some more time in the battle simulator, my young warrior!" In *MYST*, you got to stumble around a deserted island for days, looking for the barbecue you knew everyone else must be attending—until you began to wonder whether something might be amiss in this strange world, and went out and bought the hint book.

Naturally, *MYST*'s unbelievable success spawned a series of imitators, all combining beautifully rendered 3-D graphics with spooky backstories, eerie animations, and mind-bending puzzles and mysteries. The best of the post-*MYST* games was *The 7th Guest*, in which you had to unravel a macabre mystery before it unraveled you. The worst was a game called *Guess What Bad Thing Happened Here a*

Long Time Ago, in which you had to answer a few knock-knock jokes to discover the location of some missing car keys.

Parents' Games

Many parents were alarmed when their children's mastery of games like *Doom* included being able to code and insert their own *Doom* scenarios, levels, and especially monsters—many of which bore uncomfortable resemblances to the kids' parents, teachers, older siblings, and schoolmates. The parents' dismay was short-lived, however, when they turned the same technology to their own advantage, coming up with versions of games that featured massacres of Barney, Big Bird, Madeline, Power Rangers, Ninja Turtles, and Shari Lewis. With children digitally destroying their elders, and parents virtually vaporizing their kids' idols, the resulting catharsis brought about a nationwide detente between young and old.

Dull, Dull, Dull, Dull but Useful Software

Every so often, your hand will cramp around the joystick as you're getting your space-pilot's ass kicked by a clan of slimy alien critters. Instead of switching to a game in which you get your explorer's ass chewed off by a clan of subterranean mutant critters, take a look at the useful software that was pre-loaded on your computer. Some of these programs can maul your ass faster than any critter. Don't worry if you never master most of them, either—in order to do that, you'd have to read each application's manual. And since each program comes with a manual between two hundred and eight hundred pages long, and you have a hard time concentrating long

---

Three Game-Inspired Ideas That Never Made It

1. *Doom:* The Theme Park
2. The *Mortal Kombat* Cookbook
3. SimCologne

---

enough to fill out the registration card, it would take a miracle for you to make it through any of them. The most you can hope to do is learn just enough to demonstrate your mastery to someone else, and make them feel stupid.

Financial Software

A truly scary idea. With one easy click, you could wipe out your entire retirement plan (if you had one), sell all your stocks at a loss (if you owned any), and zero out your checking account balance (if you weren't already running in the red). What makes these programs useful? They're tax-deductible. And since yours came with the computer, you can deduct not only the cost of the computer, but the cost of the hutch, ergonomic chair, antistatic plastic mat, Gore-Tex wrist support, beaded over-the-chair back support, uninterrupted power supply, and subscription to *Popular Mechanics* as well. You say you don't have most of that stuff? I didn't say to buy it, did I? I said to deduct it.

Speaking of deductions, don't even think about buying tax software. Yes, it may be cheaper than a tax accountant, and it might be as

---

Software Requirements

Always check the System Requirements on the software package. They tell you the minimum features your computer must have in order for that program to run. Of course, having the program "run" and having the program "work" are two completely different things. If you want a particular program to actually work on your computer, you should double the minimum RAM required. Here's what the words really mean:

Minimum: satisfies the legal definition of functionality
Recommended: essential
Enhanced: will not crash your computer
Upgrade: we think it might work now

---

knowledgeable about the code as a tax accountant, but it can't do the one thing that makes a tax accountant really valuable: lie. When you get audited, it'll be just you and your tax software sitting there, trying to explain five thousand dollars in "educational materials" with a straight face.

If you have to buy tax software, give it to your accountant. And deduct it.

Spreadsheet

Did you know that the word *spreadsheet* was around long before computers? If you didn't, just skip this kind of program entirely. You're better off with a ruler, a pencil, and a piece of paper.

Those of you who do remember having to deal with ledgers, adding machine tapes, black and red pencils, and endless special erasers know how gruesome dealing with spreadsheets used to be. *You* can appreciate the way spreadsheet programs virtually eliminated the sheer drudgery of working with numbers, and minimized the risk of human error. *You* know how much personal computing owes to applications like Lotus 1-2-3. *You* know the extent to which mankind has benefited from software that has made everything from high finance to basement inventory easier, simpler, faster, better. Unfortunately, nobody cares what *you* think. *You're* an accountant.

Word Processing

These days, just about any word processing program will enable you to compose professional-looking documents in any number of formats: newsletter, legal deposition, greeting card, outline, and plea bargain, to name just a few. What's more, you can import documents and graphics from other programs and embed them in your word processing file for impressive presentations, complete with footnotes, technical characters and symbols, color graphs, and lively sidebars.

Sounds overwhelming, doesn't it? Well, it is. If you're like most people, the tremendous capabilities built into word processing programs serve only to emphasize the painful fact that no fancy format, elegant font, or colorful layout can disguise: *you have nothing to say.*

You can, however, have fun exploring the power of your word processing program. After a little intense study, you can learn how to set your word processor options so that your printer will print as you write! This wonderful feature manages to turn your $2,500 computer into a typewriter.

Database

Database programs teach you that there are an infinite number of ways you can try to look up who gave you the Deepak Chopra quilt for your wedding. You can:

- Query about "Chopra"

- Generate a report about "Bad Gifts"

- List all the "Presents to Get Rid of After the Giver Dies"

- Seek under "Idiot"

- Find "All anagrams of *Koch Appeared*"

Personal Organizer

Personal organizers can alert you to the fact that you should put out the Deepak Chopra quilt today, because your brother-in-law is coming over.

Fax Managers

Fax managers are by far the cruelest software of all. They generate scary file names like ~00__0020.f?x. They print out scary commands like ATMODT and ATHO+++ and A&F&A&P&B#&Bb&H1&R2&D2&C3P0&4S0=0S7=90. And when you've given up trying to make them work, they start answering the phone for you. What's more, since you can never manage to send a fax on the first try, you and the faxee have to have a prearranged protocol in the event of failure. Otherwise, he answers the phone whenever you're trying to resend the fax, and he lets his computer answer whenever you want to talk to him, and each of you ends up trying to talk to a remote computer by imitating the sound of the modem.

CAD (Computer Aided Design)

Maybe you're thinking about building a house or adding an extension. Perhaps you simply want to rearrange the furniture in your living room, and want to know, without lifting a finger, if it is possible to switch the sideboard and the china cabinet. A CAD program can answer all your design questions.

Oh yeah—you'll need a digitizing pad and wireless mouse, a 133 Mhz job with 128 MB RAM, and an advanced engineering degree from MIT. Otherwise, stick with your kid's Crayola program.

Language Programs

Can you learn French, German, Italian, Spanish—even Chinese and Japanese—from a computer program? One of the leading manufacturers of such language software replies:

> Powerful multimedia computers—with their incredible speed, memory, and accessibility—have completely transformed what it means to learn a foreign language. Just one CD-ROM contains months of classroom experience—not just vocabulary builders and pronunciation guides, but interactive dialogues, challenging games, and cultural and historical information as well. This is multimedia at its best—without leaving your home, you can completely immerse yourself in the language of your choice.

If, after reading the above, you still think you can learn Mandarin Chinese just by double-clicking on an icon of the Great Wall, you need to brush up on your English.

Graphics

Using the latest paint, draw, or photoshop program is a truly religious experience. These programs give you a level of choice and control that is unprecedented in the history of human endeavor. Editing and effects menus beget other submenus, which in turn beget generations of pop-ups, further begetting clickable option boxes with preview screens, color charts, and other mind-numbing possibilities. There are simply so many choices—so many more than anyone has ever had to cope with—that one's tendency is to ignore 95 percent of the editing options, rather than have to select one thing to do from among thousands of choices. After mucking about with one of these programs, it's easy to understand how some omnipotent being might create the universe and then just leave it alone, paralyzed into inaction by the staggering number of possibilities.

Screen Saver

Never has so much money been invested in showing the world how little you're getting done. The first screen savers were small buttons near the base of the monitor that, when depressed, blanked the screen by blocking the electrical current powering the monitor. Known as on-off switches, they were replaced by much less labor-intensive software solutions, known as screen savers. These programs displayed showy, often moving, images after a predetermined number of minutes had lapsed with no input from the user. Screen savers thus perform two functions: 1) they prevent any continuously displayed image from being permanently "burned" on the monitor screen, and 2) they terrify the daydreaming user into action by suddenly displaying pictures of William Shatner, David Hasselhoff, and Barney.

Project Management Software

The ultimate in organizational tools, project management programs lay out in incredible detail the resources, timetable, and budget needed to accomplish anything from relocating a residence to building a space station. So detailed, so comprehensive are these programs that the budgets and timetables they produce are almost always accurate to within 1 percent. (To be fair, some of the accuracy can be attributed to the fact that because it takes so long to master the software, most project management documents are written three weeks after the project has already been completed.)

Don't Be Scared!

Many have ascribed the recent drop in software sales to the fact that software titles are just too intimidating. Titles like Excel, Quicken, and WordPerfect just aren't appropriate to most users' level of computer savvy. In response, developers are repackaging some of their standard titles under alternate names. Here's the key:

Standard Title	Alternate Title
Lotus 1-2-3	Muddle Through
Quicken	Eke!
WordPerfect	Scribble
Doom	Ouch
Director	Lackey

File and Disk Utilities

Unlike all the previous software, file and disk utility programs have clear, concise commands that are easily understood, like Move, Copy, and Delete. Because of this clarity, most people gravitate to utility programs when they're just learning how to use a computer—and within just a short while, they're happily deleting their config.sys and renaming all those pesky batch files.

Recent Software Trends

Lately, a group of software manufacturers has taken the view that applications, instead of being sleek and elegant tools, have become unwieldy, memory-guzzling extravaganzas designed not to address a particular need or market, but to demonstrate the technical superiority of their programmers. These manufacturers have taken this view not so much because it's the truth, but because there's a buck in it for them. Realizing that every significant socioeconomic movement creates its own backlash, these savvy software developers are hard at work developing what they like to call "lean" software.

Lean software will be simpler to use, make fewer demands on system resources, and have far fewer complex features than today's software behemoths. In fact, most lean software won't even take up any room on your hard drive. Lean software will run right from your floppy disk drive! Naturally, lean software will be as expensive as monster programs, but only until the research and development costs have been recouped by the manufacturers of lean software.

Most of the research money will go toward figuring out how to make sure nobody realizes that lean software is nothing more than "really old" software.

Shareware

At first, "shareware" sounds like a remarkable utopian concept, a benefit to mankind and the last bastion of goodness. Friendly programmers around the world develop and distribute their own applications, free of charge! All you have to do is download them from an online service or bulletin board, or copy them from friends, and there you are! Free stuff!

What you need to know about shareware is that there is only one guy who actually writes good shareware and gives it away. He is a fervent opponent of copyrighted software. He is the Mother Teresa of the computer world. He is noble, he is good, and he is destined to fade into oblivion. His name is . . . oh, well.

All the other shareware is written by programmers who can't quite get anything right, can't quite spell anything right, and have an inappropriate confidence in their sense of humor. They all share a peculiar fondness for garish graphics best suited to upholstery found in a recreational vehicle and spend most of their programming energy coming up with that irritating box that keeps asking you to register your shareware.

A word about registering shareware: Almost every shareware program posts a friendly message that follows this format:

This shareware version of PONZI PRO PLUS is to be used for evaluation only. You may use it for 30 days. If, after 30 days, you want to continue receiving two dollars from thousands of strangers, you must register your copy of PONZI PRO PLUS. There is a small registration fee of $19.95. Once you have registered, you will receive your licensed version of PONZI PRO PLUS, which includes features unavailable in the shareware version: the PYRAMID Financial Schemer and Planner, a searchable listing of Psychic Hot Lines, and plot synopses from the second season of "Quantum Leap."

Register		OK

You are on day **257** of your evaluation period.

Byte Me!

This message pops up every time you start the program, in order to remind you what a jerk you are for reneging on your promise to abide by the terms of use, laid out in the unread README.TXT you downloaded along with the program. But the reminder isn't the most important part of the registry message—the *counter* is. To most shareware users, the counter is more than just an unsettling reminder that they are cheating. It's a sign that someone else knows what they're doing. The program knows. And the higher that counter gets, the more positive the cheater becomes that there's a little switch in the program, some little line of code that says "IF EVAL   DAY = 257," the program will branch off to a little function that attaches a virus to your command.com before resuming normal operation. For the next two weeks the program runs as usual, but all the while that little virus is chipping away at the computer, setting up a complex operation to domino through every program and file—until day 300, when the computer displays the following message when booting:

```
                config.sys not found
                please wait ...........................
......................................................
......................................................
......................................................
......................................................
....while I delete everything on the hard dri-
ve ............. no, ⟨Esc⟩ won't work .............
.........neither will the power switch.........
............................... no, pulling the
plug won't work, because I'm using only the power
```

```
stored in your CMOS battery......................
................hasta la vista................
................................................
................................................
................................................
.......................................baby
```

Of course, such fears are completely groundless.

Chapter 9

When Something Goes Wrong

The first time you have a problem with your new computer, your initial reaction will be to ignore it. It might go away by itself. Of course, only once in the entire history of electronics has a problem gone away by itself, but who knows? This just might be the second time. But if, after several hundred crashes, thirty-odd file linkages, and nine outbursts of "I've had it with this piece of crap!" you think the problem still exists, here are the correct questions to ask:

Can I fix it myself?

Of course not—not unless the problem turns out to be that you had the keyboard upside down.

What does the manual say?

Your trusty manual provides helpful answers, tips, and tricks, but . . .

Where the heck did I put the manual?

Unfortunately, the last place most people keep their manuals is near their computers. They feel it makes them look digitally inept.

Which manual should I look in?

Having more than one manual is a problem unless you know what caused the trouble in the first place. Let's see: Is a mid-program dump to a flashing hyphen on a blank screen with a simultaneous keyboard freeze caused by an application error? Is it caused by an operating system error? Could it be somehow related to that grinding sound coming from the hard drive?

What do I call this problem?

Once you decide which manual to consult, you have to be able to recognize the problem in the manual's troubleshooting guide. While this may sound daunting at first, it really isn't. Although there are hundreds of potential problems listed in every troubleshooting guide, there are only two recommended courses of action, both of which translate to "You're an idiot":

1. Make sure the unit is plugged in.

2. Make sure the unit is turned on.

After the entire section, it says "If you have followed the recommended procedures and the trouble persists, please contact Technical Support (anyone's but ours)."

Where do I find the Technical Support number?

Good question. Computer dealers know they have to have Technical Support numbers, but they try to keep the number of actual callers down—not by selling quality goods, but by hiding the Technical Support number among dozens of other numbers you'd never want to call. The trick to recognizing a Technical Support number is spotting the sentence that follows it: "Have your serial number handy when you call."

Now just try to find your serial number.

Getting in Touch with Technical Support

There will come a time when you will need to contact your manufacturer's Technical Support team. For most users, this is approximately seven minutes after unpacking the computer. The manufacturer's Technical Support number is almost never an 800 number, and is always a long distance call. Before you call the Technical Support line, have the following items ready:

1. Your computer's model number

2. Your computer's serial number

3. Your receipt

4. A good book

Preparing for the Worst

One day, usually about a week after your warranty expires, some piece of hardware in your computer will simply break, and you'll wonder what to do. You have three choices:

1. Contact an authorized computer repair center.
2. Ask a knowledgeable friend—say, the guy down the street who built his own lawnmower.
3. Turn the CPU upside down, shake it a few times, and see if that fixes it.

The answer is, of course,

4. Abandon ship. Get everything useful you can off of your computer, and get rid of it. Take it to the nearest dump, dumpster, Salvation Army donation bin, or river, and throw it in. Then run. Run just as fast as you can. Once a computer has gone bad, there is no hope of salvation. The only thing you can do is make sure it doesn't infect the rest of your equipment.

You might have noticed that it's easier to track down Sasquatch than it is to locate a live Technical Support human on one of these help lines. The reason for this is obvious: live technical people mean live payrolls, and live health insurance, and live 401(k) plans, and live sexual harassment suits . . . and nobody wants that kind of thing anymore. Understanding this fact will help you negotiate your way through Technical Support. Simply remember the Golden Rule of Customer Service: You Are a Pest.

To keep you away from them, most Technical Support people institute an automated system to detour your call. A typical message runs:

"Welcome to the NOMAD Industries Technical Support Line. Your call is important to us. Please listen to the following choices, and push the number corresponding to your choice. If you do not have a push button phone, perhaps you should have considered getting one before you bought a computer.

If you would like to order a NOMAD Industries product, press 1.

If you are having trouble installing NOMAD Software, press 2.

If you are having trouble configuring NOMAD Software, press 3.

If you are having trouble opening up the NOMAD Software package, press 4.

If you don't understand the difference between Riker's job and Picard's job, press 5.

If you need to speak to a member of our Technical Support staff, press the % button.

The current Technical Support calling queue is beyond human comprehension."

Recent consumer periodicals and newspaper stories report that the computer industry's Technical Support systems have undergone drastic improvements. This just goes to show that even Tech Support managers know how to hire press agents.

Getting Even with Technical Support

After several futile calls to Technical Support, you're going to feel an overpowering desire to destroy the equanimity of the tech people who have made your life a living nightmare. Have you ever noticed that tech people like to ask a lot of "yes or no" questions?

This is to eliminate unnecessary, mistaken, and misleading statements you might make. Here's a fun little game to play with them.

First, grab a coin. Then, call up your favorite Tech Support sadist and complain that your computer crashes whenever you double-click on the program icon. After a drawn-out sigh of forbearance, the tech guy will start asking you questions. All you have to do is answer them according to the following rules:

Whenever he asks a "yes or no" question, flip the coin and answer "yes" if the coin comes up heads, "no" if it comes up tails.

Whenever he asks you to read exactly what's on the screen, say "Okay, there's a little . . . the screen just went blank again!"

If you don't have that kind of time to spend on petty revenge, try this one: take out a help-wanted ad in *USA Today* for "Night Janitor Wanted at United States Mint. Must be able to work alone." Refer interested parties to your favorite 800 Technical Support number.

Mum's the Word

If you ever happen to figure out one of cyberspace's great mysteries—say, how to change program icons—you might be tempted to tell a few of your friends. Don't. Don't ever tell anyone you know about anything you've managed to achieve with your computer, because that will automatically make you the Designated Computer Tutor of your circle. For the next decade you'll be deluged with all sorts of questions from friends who want to jump on the digital bandwagon:

- Should I get a Mac or an IBM?
- What's RAM?
- What's a hard drive?
- What's a floppy?
- Will you come with me?
- Will you buy it for me?

Avoid this trouble by never being the first on your block to do anything, buy anything, or try anything connected with computers. As Buffalo Bills head coach Marv Levy can tell you, coming in second means you miss out on the glory—but at least your evenings are your own.

Chapter 10

Multimedia

Ask someone in the business about the so-called new art form inspired by multimedia. You will hear frequent pauses, see a lot of gestures, and encounter words like *synthesis*, *paradigm*, and *interactive*. Although no one seems to know where multimedia is heading, everyone is positive that it's going to involve new forms of social, political, and artistic endeavor and forever change the face of human existence. So far, all it has managed to do is introduce the phrase "cheat keys" into the English language. In fact, multimedia has recently ceded its role as Savior of the Civilized World and Transcendental Glory of Our Future to the World Wide Web (of which more later).

The foundation of multimedia is the CD-ROM, that miraculous disk capable of holding huge amounts of data. For all its wonders, the one thing everyone wants to know is: How do I grab the thing? By the sides? Which side can't I touch? Which side is the magic side? Relax. If you saw how these things get thrown around at multimedia companies, you'd realize they're about as delicate as a soap dish. The jokers who make them just get a kick out of knowing that you treat these indestructible plastic things as if they were soufflés.

What Is Multimedia?

The CD-ROM (Compact Disk Read Only Memory) made it possible for tremendous amounts of data to be stored on one disk—not only standard text files, but memory-hogging sound and video files as well. Suddenly it was feasible to produce programs that involved not just one of our senses, but *two*!

Multimedia was immediately hailed as a miraculous development, mostly by people who never thought to turn the radio on while working at the computer. Today, almost every PC is a multimedia computer, and the CD is fast replacing the floppy disk as the medium of choice for just about any application.

Today's multimedia computers employ three distinct types of activity—seeing, hearing, and typing—to transform personal computing from a dry, repetitive chore into a dry, repetitive interactive musical experience.

Big Deal

Like every other consumer of multimedia goods, you have no doubt marveled at the amount of multimedia junk flooding the marketplace. It's a shame that you never get to see one of these wonderful products as originally envisioned: cross-platform, innovative, interactive, and absorbing; a continually surprising, ever-changing tour-de-force of modern technology and future potential. What you get is what's left of this vision after periodic budget cutbacks, ornery programming myopia, editorial indecision, and inattentive executive meddling have worked their magic on it. That's why the most impressive feature of any finished multimedia product is its advertising.

This all started way back in the late 1980s, when multimedia was proclaimed the Official Future of Personal Computing and Savior of Civilization. In a mad rush to capture this burgeoning market, everyone on the planet formed a multimedia company and started spitting out CD-ROM titles. The gap between technological potential and market reality was staggering, leading to the first great Multimedia Age, the Era of Undefined Dynalinks. Some of the less-than-inspired titles issued during this period include *The Multimedia Helen Keller*, *The CD-ROM Guide to Alpaca*, and *Steal This CD-ROM*.

A period of readjustment followed, during which all but twenty-three multimedia companies bit the dust. The survivors realized it was going to take a little more than the label "Multimedia!" to sell

titles—it was going to take hyperbole. Thus began the second great Multimedia Age, the Era of Shameless Superlatives, which saw the release of such titles as *The Absolutely Essential Bob Saget, The Compleat Lug Nut Companion,* and *The Indexed, Annotated, Explicated, and Extrapolated Multimedia Lincoln Log Handbook.* This round of production wiped out all but eleven multimedia companies. These hardy survivors had learned their lesson. The public wanted more out of multimedia than speedy production and hype: they wanted celebrities!

The third great Multimedia Age, The Resurrection (but known to many as "After They Were Stars"), is known primarily for its reliance on digitized video clips of ex–Love Boat guest stars to sell titles. Multimedia gamers piloted star fighters not for the glory of testing their mettle in galactic combat, but for a swell pat on the back from Mark Hamill. (It quickly became standard practice, after a successful mission, for players to hit their fighter's self-destruct button, rather than return to base for one of Hamill's wooden compliments.) Reference works coupled fascinating topics with expert commentary as Jonathan Frakes, Morgan Fairchild, and Joe Piscopo sat down to play poker together—one title that would have benefited from a self-destruct button.

Only five multimedia companies survived this round of consumer ambush. Realizing the consequences of another misstep, they desperately sought the ingredient that had been missing from their titles. After much angst and research, they were stunned to discover that the public wanted something entirely unexpected: they wanted substance.

Today we are witnessing the Age of Content Wars. All over the globe, multimedia companies are scrambling to buy up the rights to anything that qualifies as "content": books, movies, television shows, music, magazines, games, photographs, matchbook covers, warning labels attached to pillows, and liner notes from Rick Astley albums. Once everything yet said, done, or drawn has been used on a CD-ROM, we will pass into the period everyone dreads: the Era of Created Content. Once all the existing content has been exhausted, the multimedia business will rely exclusively on content created just for CD-ROMs—a genre that has already given us such masterpieces as *Eat with Tommy Lasorda!* and *The Dalai Lama's Home Video Companion.* It will be a scary time. In fact, a core group of multimedia magnates, fearing the consequences of too much created content, has agreed to commit mass suicide should anyone release a CD-ROM with Pauly Shore's name on it.

Chapter 11

The Information Superhighway

The information superhighway is, first and foremost, a toll road. It seems we weren't spending enough money on computers, monitors, ergonomic keyboards, printer stands, CD organizers, floppy disk wallets, work stations, Dust-Off, scanners, sound cards, joysticks, glare filters, and hinged copy holders that velcro right onto the side of your monitor until you actually attach a piece of paper to it, at which point the whole thing comes tearing off. No, we needed another outlet for all that money we'd socked away for retirement. We needed the "Information Superhighway"!

Futurists predict that the day will come when we can carry out all of our interpersonal transactions (okay, most of them) through our personal computers. Instead of lugging textbooks to school and back every day, we'll have the entire school curriculum on-line, where we can ignore it even more easily than we do now. We won't even have to break the spines of our books to make it look like we've done the reading. And all our banking will be done over high-speed phone lines, giving rise to a new generation of transparent excuses for evading payment: "Geez, I sent that in yesterday! What's your e-mail address? Oh, I thought it was loandept@chem*bark*.com."

The most dramatic effect is already being seen in the way we work, as telecommuting becomes more and more widespread. Conferences, reviews, and water cooler slamfests can now be done electronically, through e-mail or videoconferencing. Documents make the rounds through networks, obviating the need for hard copy of rough drafts. From laptops, notebooks, and desktops across the country and around the world, employees are able to execute their tasks with a new comfort and freedom unimaginable just a few short years ago. Today there is really only one compelling reason to collect all the employees of a company in a common workplace: you want them to actually get something done.

Today's telecommuter wakes up late, checks his e-mail, has breakfast, watches a little "Regis and Kathie Lee" just to feel superior, gets dressed, takes a cup of coffee, and wanders over to the computer. After just one game of mah-jongg, he settles in for fifty-three more games of mah-jongg, after which it's time to check e-mail again. Lunch follows, and after watching a little "Rolonda," our telecommuter opens up a spreadsheet, tries to enter a formula, and crashes his computer. He reboots, spends an hour running diagnostics and other disk utilities, and then checks to make sure everything is okay by playing fifty-three games of mah-jongg.

Recent legislative and technological advances have opened up the field of digital communications beyond telephone lines, signaling the onset of all-out warfare between the telephone companies, who currently command the market, and cable television operators, only now able to compete with phone companies for a piece of the lucrative digital pie. This kind of free-market competition is what drives prices down, research forward, and consumers out of their minds. In the near future these two giant industries will spend vast amounts of money trying to convince you to make them your information provider. Ironically, not one dollar will be spent by phone companies to fix the way call waiting always bumps your modem off-line, and the cable companies won't spend one penny to find out why your service is blacked out whenever a grouse flies past their broadcast center. That kind of stuff is too retro for such forward-looking industries.

What does the future hold for the information superhighway? To take the metaphor to a logical conclusion, the future will see a vast system of interconnected highways and byways, a global network of potential pathways to information, entertainment, education, fi-

A Word about Parental Control

Many parents are concerned about the effect computers can have on their children. How can they stay a step ahead of their kids and protect them from being exposed to bad ideas?

Good luck. The fact is, most parents are already three steps behind their kids when it comes to computers. Whereas a lot of adults still haven't gotten over the fear of computers they picked up from the movie *2001*, a lot of kids will be on their third Powerbook by that year. And as for the software that supposedly allows parents to control computer access: who do you think wrote that software? Fifteen-year-old whiz kid programmers working part time for 18-year-old multimillionaires, that's who. And shareware versions of the same software are being written by eight-year-old students in lieu of making clay ashtrays.

The only thing parents can really do is show their kids how to tell the difference between good ideas and bad ideas. In exchange, kids can explain to their parents the difference between the computer's representation of reality and reality itself.

nancial security, and just plain fun. Just like today's asphalt highways, on the information superhighway you'll be able to take the whole family on an extended getaway limited only by your imagination. And just like today, the vehicle you take will go much too slowly, no one will ever want to do the same thing, urgent trips to the bathroom will ruin your pace, and by the time you get home you won't be able to stand one another.

On-Line Services: Because You Can Never Have Too Much Artwork

On-line services are the package tours of cyberspace. Sign up, log on, and forget about your cares. Need a Web browser? Your on-line service has one ready for downloading. Want to do a little shopping? Your on-line service has its own electronic shopping mall. Want to stay in touch with your friends? Your on-line service shows you how to earn free hours by suckering your friends and family into joining. Joining one of America's premier on-line services is like joining a Great Big Family—of mercenaries.

The essential strategy of the top three on-line service providers is the same: offer the new user a good chunk of free time to explore the service; say, eight hours. Get the user to register with a credit card number for future billing, "in the unlikely event of surcharges." Then use up all but thirty seconds of that free eight hours downloading artwork, giving little tours of the service, and installing browsers and mail applications.

Here are the top three:

CompuServe

CompuServe touted itself as the serious on-line service, built for serious businessmen doing serious work and looking for some downright serious information. To show how serious they were, subscribers were given numbers, not user names. Logging in meant typing out a number like `7630482,653` and then entering a password as pleasant as `TRAPEZOID/PHLEGM`. Automating the process made it easier to log in, but the underlying seriousness remained.

125

CompuServe's own research showed that the most popular forum in its serious on-line service was the "Brown Paper Bag" section of its Graphics Plus Library, the most common character string used in its File Search utility was "supermodel," and the most visited chat channel was "Star Trek Trivia." Soon thereafter CompuServe began aping America Online's habit of using incredibly ugly icons and smarmy announcements, and *People* magazine became a regular feature. The most serious CompuServe feature, however, remained: the Extended Service clock, which begins racking up additional charges as soon as you do anything more than check your e-mail.

CompuServe's navigation command is GO. You can GO GAMERS to enter an area dedicated to games, or GO SOAPFORUM to learn about various soap operas, or GO INTERNET to reach any one of the Net services CompuServe provides. If you want to complain about how much you're being charged for those ubiquitous extended services, you pretty much know where you can GO.

Prodigy

You won't be surprised to hear that Prodigy's interface was designed by a blind schizophrenic with fluorescent crayons. Somehow, the folks over there equated user-friendly with ugly-wugly, and came up with a GUI that even billboard painters hate. Still, it is a customizable ugly interface—subscribers can choose which garish colors will greet them each time they log on, or select one of four different fonts:

- A standard ugly font

- A bigger, uglier version of the same font

- A really big, ugly version of the same font

- An extremely big and ugly version of the same font

Prodigy's most notable feature is its love affair with the scroll bar. Almost everywhere you go there are three scrollable boxes of text for you to play with. Sometimes there is a list of options with only two items, and the list is still scrollable. Prodigy's navigational command, JUMP, is inelegant but the guy who runs it is a big Van Halen fan.

America Online

America Online is the current champion among on-line services, which makes it easily the most detested as well. The sorry truth is that the more members you have, the more morons you have. America Online is best known for its inability to leave well enough alone. Every three minutes or so every AOL feature gets a completely new set of what AOL likes to call artwork, a process that eats up twenty minutes of on-line time, and re-places amateurish-looking happy icons with 3-D rendered ama-teurish-looking happy icons. AOL likes to point out that all the download time is free, as if you have nothing better to do than watch a little download-status bar creep its way across your screen.

AOL is renowned for its ubiquitous free software disks, given away with computing magazines, bundled with new computer systems, and distributed by helicopter over parts of Bosnia. Installing the software and joining AOL are as easy as slipping the disk in your computer and running the install program—in contrast to the Her-culean effort it takes to cancel your AOL membership, which re-quires the following:

- An on-line notice of cancellation

- A phone call to the outfit's overburdened 800 number

- A post card mailed to AOL president Steve Case with the words "take a hike, sonny" somewhere in the body of the message

- An officially sanctioned AOL exorcism performed by a duly trained priest, rabbi, minister, or any original cast member of *Baa, Baa, Black Sheep*

America Online doesn't have a navigation command, because AOL doesn't demand that its subscribers be familiar with arcane terms like GO and JUMP.

One of AOL's remarkable flashes of genius is an area of Member Services in which AOL subscribers try to help other AOL subscribers: suggesting solutions to their problems, offering tips, sharing ways to navigate the on-line service. AOL suggests that members with questions try this avenue first, rather than bother AOL technicians who actually have the answers. It's another way of making new friends by discovering a common bond: hatred of AOL.

What's the Difference?

Each on-line service offers its own uniquely irritating personality. CompuServe is as exciting as any company owned by H&R Block could ever be. Prodigy is as friendly, accessible, and meaningful as graffiti scrawled on a rest room wall. And becoming a member of America Online has the same comfortable, personal, down-home feeling you get in Times Square on New Year's Eve.

The future of on-line services is pretty cloudy. Its main attraction, after all, is packaging content and services under one roof, with a free software package to match (these days, even Jehovah's Witnesses tote around free software disks for America Online). But as Web browsing software gets easier to use and more comprehensive in the number of functions it can perform, more people will turn to companies that simply provide a connection to the Internet.

Bulletin Boards: When Amber Monitors Are Too Showy

Bulletin boards are the treehouses of the nineties. Before the Internet became accessible to the general consumer, bulletin boards were the hottest things around. Thousands of computer owners threw a few dedicated phone lines into home units set in Host mode, announced the existence of the Agronomy BBS, and started signing up members, usually for free. Nowadays, bulletin boards have been reduced to filling specialized roles, most of them either dull or criminal, sometimes both (the Jaywalkers' BBS comes to mind). But the future is bright for these graphically challenged dinosaurs. As nitwit government zealots hastily throw together hypocritical and ultimately unconstitutional legislation to limit expression on the Internet, people will increasingly seek refuge in the private bulletin boards they abandoned. The Web will gradually assume the cultural, artistic, and intellectual character of Nazi Germany, while bulletin boards will form a kind of underground Resistance.

Internet Providers

For people interested primarily in what the Internet offers, a full-service on-line account—for instance, with CompuServe or AOL—may be prohibitively expensive. Browsing the World Wide Web from an on-line service, for even an hour a day, can run up connect

129

bills in excess of this year's NEA budget. In addition, on-line services often avoid controversy by restricting access to "sensitive" areas of the Internet and policing the content of member forums and chats. For complete access to the Internet without interference or censorship, many people opt to use an Internet provider—a service that, for a flat fee, provides you with little more than a direct link to the Internet.

Thousands of Internet providers have sprung up over the last year both to address the demand for direct Internet access and to give incompetent techies a way to make a living. You see, Internet provider is to the computer industry what "E!" entertainment reporter is to journalism: a job you end up with when nothing else is working for you. Those who lack even the minimal creativity to design Websites and the minimal technical expertise to produce hardware become Internet providers. It only takes a few dozen phone lines, an Internet connection, and a couple of newspaper ads to get started.

Internet providers are invariably local businesses (to make logging on a local call), so they have to live with the danger that a customer might actually stop by for a look and discover a) how junky the equipment really is, b) how few people actually work there, and c) how few of those people are over the age of fifteen. To minimize this threat, most IP offices are double-locked, unlabeled, and open only from 10 a.m. to 3 p.m. If by some miracle you do happen to get in during these hours, a shrill office manager will inform you that, regrettably, you can't see the setup because "we're recalibrating one of our annexes." After you've gone, the manager will then add "recalibrating one of our annexes" to the company's list of Euphemisms for Eating Pizza.

At home, the first difference you'll notice between an Internet provider and an on-line service is in the log-on procedure. Services like Prodigy provide subscribers with a complete software package.

Questions to Ask About Your Internet Provider

Before you sign up with an Internet provider, shop around a little bit. Ask the following questions about each candidate for your dollar:

1. When you called for information, was your call answered within three rings?
2. Four rings?
3. Five?
4. Did anyone ever answer?
5. Did you sign up anyway?
6. I thought so.

Once you install the software, all you have to do is double-click on a "Connect" icon and wait until you hear the welcome announcement. If you have joined an Internet provider, however, finding and installing the software you use to connect is up to you. Sometimes your provider will suggest (or even supply) a shareware program to use; often you'll go out and buy one for yourself. Mind you, this software isn't something for navigating the Web or using e-mail; this is just a program to get you connected to the Internet through your provider. Once you've logged on, you have to use different software to navigate the Internet. And logging on looks a little different—double-click on the "Connect" icon, and watch as your log-on script runs through its paces:

```
Line busy.
Trying again . . .
Line busy.
Trying again . . .
Line busy.
Trying again . . .
Line busy.
Trying again . . .
```

After a few minutes of this, you'll be able to connect, and the following sequence will run:

```
Login . . .
User name: AlDurham
Password: ******
Logging in . . .
)&ργεтη❑♦Ω↙*^@!!%⌗⌗⌗vasthrt6hhdsgd*^>~'zP::
Disconnect
```

This line of garbage and subsequent disconnect can be caused by any number of things: a dirty phone line, a bad connection, the early onset of Alzheimer's. After about thirty minutes alternating between busy signals and disconnects, you'll finally see some variation of the following message:

```
Okay, so you made it. You're logged on. Goody for you.
What now, Einstein?
```

The Internet

The selling of the Internet is a classic in the annals of capitalism. We, the people, are more than willing to fork out big bucks for servers, providers, and software that get us hooked up to the Internet, because after all, the Internet is free! The Internet is a utopian, free-form marketplace of ideas where information is freely exchanged, all men and women are created equal, and God doesn't play dice.

Isn't it?

Well, no. The Internet began as a Defense Department project, which means not only that it has been paid for many, many, many times over with your tax dollars, but also that it could have been designed and set up for thirty-seven bucks in three weeks by a couple of telephone repairmen. It proved so successful that the government abandoned it, and the Internet became the clubhouse of choice for brilliant academic misfits who saw it not just as an efficient and far-ranging means of exchanging information, but as something better to do than work or study. Then, just a few years ago, the capitalists moved in and made it a going concern, building public companies, new markets, hungry consumers, and personal fortunes from a chaotic network. And as soon as the Internet became a free-market success, the government wanted back in, and the academics wanted both the government and the capitalists out.

Who's going to win? The guys with the most money, of course.

The Best Way to Get Rich through the Internet

1. Using whatever method you want—search engine, Internet White Pages, whatever—compile a list of 10,000 e-mail addresses.
2. Post the following message to everyone on the list:

   I know who you are. I saw what you did. Fifty thousand dollars to (address) by (date) or the cops find out about it.

   —the guy with the binoculars

3. Collect your dough!

Once and for All, Exactly What Is the Internet?

Okay, here we go. Once upon a time the Defense Department wondered just what the heck would happen if somebody nuked one of its strategic bases here in the U.S. of A.—for example, the Intercontinental Ballistic Missile Spell Check Room near Titusville, New Jersey. (Inside of this room sits a guy with a dictionary, a globe, and a computer terminal. In the event of nuclear warfare, it is his job to look up the spelling of all the places we're bombing, and make sure it's Asia's Georgia we want to vaporize, not Ray Charles's.) They realized that knocking out the ICBMSCR would sever an important link in its communications chain. Every piece of information routed through that room would be lost, and the resulting loss of communications could effectively paralyze the country. This tactical weakness (in military terms, an "oopsie") had to be resolved.

The department, after a few decades and a few trillion dollars worth of research, decided to decentralize its operations. Every one of the country's strategic computers, instead of just being hooked up to main defense control, was hooked up to every other strategic computer. Information sent out was no longer given specific routing directions ("go from Washington to Salt Lake City to Los Angeles"), but told only its destination ("get to Los Angeles as fast as you can"). If Salt Lake City still existed, the information might decide to get to Los Angeles that way. If Salt Lake City had been destroyed, the information would simply take the next best available route to deliver its message to Los Angeles.

The Defense Department's partners in building this system were the educational and scientific communities who not only pioneered the technology and protocol for the new network of computer communications but enjoyed the ability to easily transmit large amounts of data, exciting new theories and ideas, discussions of technique and equipment, and tofu recipes. This network of research institutions, universities, and the military, dubbed ARPANET (after Hans Arp, who the Pentagon mistakenly believed was a data, not dada, artist), was initially a success. Communications improved vastly under the system, which eliminated data transmission bottlenecks that had slowed down earlier methods of communicating. It wasn't long, however, before someone in the military questioned the advisability of having the country's defense system connected, however tenuously, to the computer science class at Felix Dzershinsky University in Moscow. The defense gang put up a bunch of electronic walls, restricted access, and pretty much left the new network of computers to the students and scientists.

Naturally, the students and scientists knew who Hans Arp was, so they held a worldwide contest to rename their network. Over half a million students, scientists, technicians, and researchers were asked to "suggest a title for the system that reflects a) its groundbreaking role in the sociological, political, and economic history of the world; b) the diverse intellectual and creative make-up of its core membership; and c) the unquenchable sense of wonder shared by all involved in the unending pursuit of truth." Entries were transmitted over a six-month period, and a special panel of judges was asked to sort through the results and, after two months of judging, announce which of the many entries would be the name of their network. They made short work of it since, of the 672,344 people who responded, 672,342 came up with "Internet." One person suggested "Ron." The remaining entry proved somewhat controversial. Half of the panel thought it a very odd, very long, very clumsy title, but still worth considering; the other half believed it was simply a plea for money to help pay for an injured stray dog's medical treatment. In the end, the panel disqualified the entry but sent off a check for ten dollars. Internet it was.

What Happened Next, Daddy?

For a few blissful years, the Internet was a global clubhouse for geeks, hackers, and brains. Since all they wanted to do was send e-mail and transfer a lot of useful data, they used transfer protocols that were lean, efficient, and unexciting—no flashy interfaces, no groovy icons, no color graphics. Few people were willing to join the Internet if it meant having to master one awkward protocol for file transfers, one for string searchers, one for e-mail, one for logging on and off, and so on. It was too much work. It was hard to grasp. Most of all, it was dull.

After a few ill-advised attempts at making the Internet more accessible (it was actually renamed "Ron" for a couple of days, just to see if that helped), in the late eighties a computer programmer named H.R. "Jim" Mengele came up with a programming language that would merge Internet services, protocols, and data into attractive, easy-to-grasp pages. These pages could eventually add graphics, sound, even animation—turning the Internet into a global network accessible and useful to anyone with a computer, a modem, and a few days to kill (modems were even slower back then). His way of formatting the Internet would turn it, he said in a now-famous speech at MIT, into a "Global Gathering Group." Thankfully, no one liked his nomenclature, and his creation was called the World Wide Web by everyone (except one idiot who insisted on calling it "World Wide Ron").

What You Can Do on the Internet

For all its bells and whistles, what you can do on the Internet is visit other computers. Guess what? Most of them are like yours, and the ones that aren't have security features to keep you out.

The Second Best Way to Get Rich through the Internet

1. Using whatever method you want—search engine, Internet White Pages, whatever—compile a list of 10,000 e-mail addresses.
2. Post the following message to everyone on the list:

    Send me a dollar.
    (P.O. Box #)
    (City, State)

3. Collect your dough!

Who's in Charge of the Internet, Anyway?

You might think that such an important concern as the Internet would be under the control of rich, influential people. It isn't. It doesn't need to be. As long as you remain under the control of rich, influential people, there's no need to control the Internet. So far, you haven't been complaining (well, there was that Ross Perot third party scare, but it passed).

F U KN REDE THS U KN KMMUNKATE N TH INTRNT :)

It's ironic that communicating on the Internet, which requires a whole bunch of typing, is populated by people who can't seem to locate the backspace key on their keyboard. In fact, the Information Revolution is responsible for more miscommunication than Isaac the bartender on "The Love Boat." This comes as no surprise—typing is, after all, a skill, one that no one in the world seems too eager to learn (at least not until Mavis Beacon picks up a BFG9000 and starts smoking cacodaemons). As a result we end up with acronyms, tortured semiphonetic spelling, and emoticons, and it all looks like the lyrics to a Dave Matthews song. It's pretty obvious that by the time voice recognition software can tell the difference between *threw* and *through*, we won't be able to. As for the Apple Newton, all those folks have to do now is hold their ground until we dumb down our literacy level to the Nootin's present capabilities.

In any event, you're going to have to learn how to communicate using all this butchered language, so here's a convenient primer for you.

ACRONYMS Use these indiscriminately—as a substitute for writing out a common phrase (IMHO—"In My Humble Opinion"), or simply as a lazy but useful habit (ICMIBIHJWMHCDTWI—"I Couldn't Make It Because I Had Just Washed My Hair and Couldn't Do a Thing with It"). The most important are:

IMHO	In My Humble Opinion
MSCL	My So-Called Life
AOL	Hell
LOL	Laughed Out Loud
ROFL	Rolled on the Floor Laughing
FOFL	Fell on the Floor Laughing
FELOFL	Fell Easily Laughing on the Floor during Greek Lunch
LFNT	There's a Huge Grey Animal Here

EMOTICONS The people who came up with these are undoubtedly the offspring of those scintillating wits who figured out how to write HELLO on the early Texas Instrument calculators.

:)	Happy
:(	Unhappy
%#&@%?$	Really Unhappy
lkjhfrd	I have a cat that likes to walk on my keyboard

INGLSH Inglsh is the language we're going to end up with after a few hundred million people get through trying to peck out messages to one another. English, which has always been hailed as a living, evolving language—usually by people who can't spell worth a damn—will be reduced to the kind of expression once seen only in cloying yearbook inscriptions like 2GOOD 2B 4GOT10. Already the effects can be seen—in Van Halen's album "OU812," the proliferation of vanity plates, and dictionaries' swelling to include more and more words as "variations in spelling (*immediatley* instead of *immediately*, *cuz* instead of *because*, *Y Kant Tori Read* instead of *Why Can't Tori Sing*). And soon you'll be able to forget there ever was such a thing as an apostrophe.

Our schools, colleges, and universities have begun to accept the inevitable deterioration of the language; in fact, fifteen states have officially dumped the three R's (Reading, Riting, and Rithmetic) for the R, the S, and the B (Reading, Spell checking, and Backing-Up). It won't be long before some instructor stands before his class, and asks if anyone wants to talk about the classic quotation on the blackboard:

2B R NOT 2B.
THTS ?

E-mail

If you think e-mail is wonderful now, just wait until collection agencies figure out how to use it. You'll be changing your Internet address more often than you change your socks. But you probably don't even think e-mail is wonderful now. You probably have it at work, which means you already know how easy it is to turn a new communications tool into a source of recrimination, misery, and deceit. Nevertheless, you're going to have to get used to it, so why not get good at it? The least you can do is learn how to cc: all the misery that comes your way.

The bad thing about e-mail is that it's really, really, really, really easy to send. Once you're on line, or networked, it only takes a second to knock off a note to someone. Why is this a bad thing? Well, if you're not getting any mail now, you can always tell yourself that people are just too lazy to sit down, write out a letter, buy stamps, find your address, and mail the damn thing. But if you never get any e-mail, it can only be because there isn't a single soul in the entire world who has anything to say to you. The easy way to get around this is to subscribe to a bunch of e-mail lists from businesses—that way there's always something in your in-box, and you've managed to avoid that loser label.

Let's take a look at a typical piece of e-mail, and break it down into its constituent parts.

```
From: Al__Turing@enigma.uk.bletchley.shh
Wed, 01 Nov 42 10:51:45
To: franklinDR@whitehouse.gov,
bbaruch@bench.park, ike@eur.eto,cdGaulle@aol.com,
monty@nafrica.net, patton@slap.com
Subject: [alt.enigma.decipher]
```

```
<On Tue Oct 31 you wrote:
  What's up?>

Nothing. What's up with you?

''Why did Constantinople get the works?
  It's no one's business but the Turks.''
```

The Address

E-mail addresses follow this general format:

alderogatis@schmenken.com

alderogatis is the user's name, handle, moniker, whatever you want to call it. If it is some version of the user's actual name, it signifies a lack of imagination. If it bears no relation to the user's name, it signifies something the user thinks is hip, but is invariably tired and stupid.

@ signifies where the user is at. Address-wise, that is. This particular character is used to force people to use the Shift key on their keyboards.

schmenken identifies the place where the guy's e-mail originates, and the **.com** extension signifies the type of institution at which the address is based. There are several types of extensions:

com means a commercial entity at which employees spend 33 percent of potential company profits sending each other "News of the Weird," "Stupid but Real Headlines," Broadway show tunes with new lyrics that rip Microsoft, and acronymic responses to all of the above.

edu is an educational institution, usually taxpayer funded, at which students spend 85 percent of the school's communications budget on flame wars.

gov means a government department, branch, or cabinet, inevitably taxpayer funded, at which civil servants spend 93 cents out of every federal dollar on interstate Death Match *Doom* games and anonymous posts to alt.fan.tim-robbins.susan-sarandon.

mil is a military base, installation, Quonset hut, submarine, jeep, aircraft carrier, or Balkan country at which our men in uniform spend 137 percent of the Peace Dividend logging on to CNN to find out just what the heck they're supposed to be doing.

Body of Message Since the art of correspondence in the United States has long been reduced to paying Hallmark to express your deepest sentiments, e-mail must be carefully composed to avoid misconstruction. The most innocent phrase to you might sound like a pernicious accusation to your correspondent.

For example: when a woman receives a reply to an earlier message, and sees the following header:

```
<at 3.15 pm on March 17, 1996 you wrote:>
```

she is pleased that her correspondent has paid her the compliment of remembering exactly what she wrote, and when she sent the original message. A man, seeing the exact same header, feels as though he's being called to account for something, and curses the fact that he committed himself in writing. Similarly, two couples arranging dinner might exchange the following:

SENT	UNDERSTOOD
1: Where do you want to eat?	We're indecisive.
2: We don't care.	We consider you a waste of time.
1: Do you want to meet inside the movie theater or outside?	We're hopelessly indecisive.
2: Outside.	We don't trust you to remember.

Signature Any e-mail software worth its salt gives you the opportunity to add a signature—like "Why did Constantinople get the works? It's no one's business but the Turks"—to all of the e-mail you send. Each piece of e-mail that you send will append this signature, individualizing what is a pretty stale format. In our example, the correspondent has decided that the best display of individuality is a quote from someone else. It is advisable to change your signature from time to time, since even your closest friends will eventually get sick of seeing "Mayonnaise makes the sandwich!" at the end of every message you send.

Replying to an E-mail Message There are those who believe that e-mail will revive the lost art of correspondence. They are sadly mistaken. One feature of e-mail ensures that well-written messages will remain a thing of the past: the fact that when you reply to a given piece of e-mail, your software automatically copies that e-mail into the body of your reply. Obviously, this is so you have a copy of the original message in front of you as you write your answer. The result is that you're no longer writing in response to a letter, you're now addressing specific queries in the message. Here's an original message, minus all the junk:

> How's it going? It seems like ages since I saw you. We've been weathering the storms here quite well; our only damage has been to Beth's tomato plants which were swallowed up by the flooded stream. Yesterday we even had some sun, so I think the worst is over and we can get back to our regular activities: bicycling. Do you remember that old red bike I had? I finally replaced it with a lime green 18-speed mountain bike, and boy what a difference!
>
> Did anything ever come of that interview you told me about? As I recall it was with some big electronics company.

Now here's the reply:

> It's going fine.
>
> It has been a long time since we saw each other.
>
> Glad to hear the weather hasn't been too bad; sad to hear about the garden.
>
> I remember that bike; I'm glad you got a new one. I can believe it's different!
>
> Nothing happened with the interview. You're right; it was with a big electronics company.
>
> Do you remember Fred? I saw him the other day.

How is your dog?

What is algae?

That's it for now!

And it doesn't stop there, as you can see by the reply to the reply:

Glad to hear it's going fine.

I remember Fred.

The dog is fine.

Algae is any plant of a group comprising seaweeds and fresh water plant life.

How is your mom?

Where were you on August 7, 1993?

Can anyone corroborate your answer?

Cheers!

Rather than revive the art of correspondence, what e-mail really does is reduce it to a strange hybrid of Gestapo interrogation and reunion chit-chat.

The real danger will come when the conventions, syntax, and format used in e-mail begin to spill over into face-to-face communication. Rather than using words to express our feelings, we'll start contorting our faces to match emoticons like :) and |: (. Our conversations will be stiff:

"Hi there! Imagine meeting you here! How are you? 'Fox hunting is the unspeakable in pursuit of the uneatable!'—Oscar Wilde."

"Hello to you! I didn't know you were in town! A moment ago, you said: <How are you?> Well, I am fine! Are you going uptown? 'Mayonnaise makes the sandwich!'—Anonymous."

"Just a second ago, you said: <Are you going uptown?> No. 'Fox hunting is the unspeakable in pursuit of the uneatable!'—Oscar Wilde."

"Just now, you said: <No.> IMHO, that's a shame. Oh well, gotta run! Bye! 'Mayonnaise makes the sandwich!'—Anonymous."

"You said: <Bye!> Bye! 'Fox hunting is the unspeakable in pursuit of the uneatable!'—Oscar Wilde."

It may well be that conversation will actually cease altogether as remote communication becomes more and more prevalent. Instead of trying to make the parties in a long-distance message, phone call, or videoconference feel as though they're all in the same place, wouldn't it be a lot easier to make in-person communication feel like it's happening at a distance? We might end up communicating solely by beaming messages back and forth between one another's palmtops. That way everyone could hear the television.

Usenet Newsgroups

Usenet is an Internet-based collection of forums, or newsgroups, for posting messages on a specific topic—for example, Charles Durning's fluctuating weight. Newsgroups are the most popular form of communication on the Net today, and will probably remain so for some time. They owe this popularity to their simplicity and their diversity. There are no fancy graphics, no applets, no plug-ins or forms in a newsgroup, just text messages. Even the binary files that when decoded become programs and graphics files are sent as text.

To participate in a newsgroup, you only need know how to read and write. As for diversity—it's enough to say that there are more than ten thousand newsgroups floating around the Net today. More are being created every day, and alt.fan.charles-durning.weight.huh hardly qualifies as one of the wackier newsgroups.

Newsgroups are categorized by interest and given prefixes that indicate the area of interest covered. The most popular are:

Prefix	Area of Interest	Example
sci	boring stuff	sci.plate-tectonics.sexy
comp	boring stuff	comp.language.really-dull.life
soc	boring liberal stuff	soc.george-will.antichrist
misc	boring miscellany	misc.jello.recipe
biz	boring stuff	biz.biz.biz.ow-a-bee.ha-ha.it's-a-joke.son
rec	boring stuff	rec.oolong.militants

The newsgroup titles themselves are fairly self-explanatory, and the only qualification for posting is that you have to behave like a complete moron. Newsgroups advertise themselves as a marketplace of ideas; what they don't tell you is that the marketplace is located in the Tower of Babel. No matter what the topic, the level of discourse in any given newsgroup is slightly lower than what you find on "The Richard Bey Show." Subscribers are always flaming one another, members of Congress, Robert T. Ironside, and—due to the proliferation of anonymous postings—often themselves. The surest way to make yourself at ease in a newsgroup is to flame America Online, its owners, customers, colors, phone numbers, logo, mailing address, and advertisements. This will get you automatic respect.

From time to time, a newsgroup will fall victim to a "Spam" war. Spamming is the posting of an advertisement to a newsgroup; most spammers post their ads to a bunch of different newsgroups, hoping to gain as wide an audience as possible. Spams are easy to spot among other newsgroup postings:

(partial listing of the newsgroup alt.fan.judicial)

Author	Subject	Date
fred@bedrock.com	re: Ito is neato . . .	1/22/96
courtney appeal	Wapner's finest moment	1/22/96
holly@miami.fla	What's a Learned Hand?	1/23/96
RICHGUY	MAKE $$$$$$ LICKING DISK LABELS!!!!!!!!!!!!!	1/23/96
waverly@uncle.gov	who's sexier: Plessy or Ferguson?	1/23/96

RICHGUY will share his easy path to wealth for a small donation to help pay his administrative costs in making such a generous offer. Unfortunately, the worst is yet to come—as they say in cyberspace, "Sometimes the flame is worse than the spam." For the next three weeks, the entire newsgroup will be paralyzed by everyone's flaming RICHGUY:

Author	Subject	Date
No6@village.org	re: MAKE $$$$$$ LICKING DISK LABELS!!!!!!!!!!!!!	1/25/96
anonymous	re: MAKE $$$$$$ LICKING DISK LABELS!!!!!!!!!!!!!	1/25/96
drain@hal.net	re: MAKE $$$$$$ LICKING DISK LABELS!!!!!!!!!!!!!	1/26/96

jluke@borg.org	re: MAKE $$$$$$ LICKING DISK LABELS!!!!!!!!!!!!!	1/27/96
ruthg@supreme.gov	Plessy was way sexier	1/31/96
pigdog	re: MAKE $$$$$$ LICKING DISK LABELS!!!!!!!!!!!!!	2/02/96
jethro@aol.com	re: MAKE $$$$$$ LICKING DISK LABELS!!!!!!!!!!!!!	2/02/96
Big G@frog.com	re: MAKE $$$$$$ LICKING DISK LABELS!!!!!!!!!!!!!	2/03/96

Ironically, most of the flames actually quote the original spam, so RICHGUY ends up getting a lot more exposure than if everyone simply ignored him. Once in a while, some peacemaker will post a message saying something like "Let's stop wasting bandwidth talking about spam!" This sensible suggestion has as much success as a U.N. peacekeeping mission. Spam wars simply have to run their course.

Sex, Sex, and More Sex If you're looking for the kind of thing that gets our patriotic, strait-laced, weak-willed, wrong-headed lawmakers in an uproar, newsgroups are the place to be. In newsgroups like alt.sex.wanted and alt.binaries.pictures.erotica, you can find everything from dominatrix lonelyhearts to doctored photographs of big-time political figures. The photographs themselves are to be found in encoded binary files which, once downloaded, can be decoded into viewable graphics files. Yes, those same little ones and zeros that help you manage your finances can arrange themselves into hot little words and pictures. If you happen to believe that the existence of these newsgroups is immoral, harmful, anti-American, and repulsive, you can pick up one of those bumper stickers that says:

IF ONES AND ZEROS WERE OUTLAWED,
ONLY OUTLAWS WOULD HAVE ONES AND ZEROS

In response to the Twitchy Prudes Lobby, the recent telecommunications bill—the one that also mandated the V-chip for all new television sets—made it illegal to transmit naughty material over the Internet where a kid might see it. One of the supporters of this kind of legislation is Donna Rice, Gary Hart's erstwhile laptop, who now pops up regularly on tabloid news shows, displaying just the kind of objectionable material she wants banned from cyberspace. You can't blame her—after the Hart business died down, her choices to get famous again were limited to getting breast implants or joining the prudes. She joined other concerned citizens of the United States who believe that giving the next generation a crippling deficit is preferable to giving them *Playboy*.

The uproar about questionable material is hardly limited to this country. Late in 1995, CompuServe yanked access to about two hundred newsgroups because they violated German obscenity laws. The Germans, who practically reinvented obscenity back in the 1930s, announced that unless German CompuServe subscribers were cut off from naughty newsgroups, CompuServe itself would be arrested, tried, convicted, and sentenced to thirty years of listening to Kraftwerk albums.

Ironically, the furor over what constitutes indecent and obscene material has made it easier for people to unknowingly stumble into material they find offensive. Members of groups like alt.sex.bondage, in order to avoid harassment by law enforcement agencies, religious zealots, and Donna Rice, have created new newsgroups with innocuous names for their postings. As a result, people checking out what's in alt.cute.bunny or rec.gregorian-chant.connoisseur might well find themselves in the middle of a flame war between amazon mud queens and galactic warrior dominatrixes.

Moderated Newsgroups A few newsgroups are moderated, which means that somebody decides which messages get posted and which don't—irrelevant messages, upsetting language, advertisements, and personal attacks are screened out; only pertinent postings using proper "netiquette" are allowed to appear. As a result, moderated newsgroups have far fewer postings with far more information about the specified topic than non-moderated newsgroups. If this makes them seem somewhat bland, they make up for it whenever a long-time member feels that the newsgroup arbiter has unjustly screened out one of his messages. That's when the veneer of civilized discourse goes out the window and the nuclear flame wars begin. The offended member challenges the arbiter's Divine Right of Moderation and begins lobbying for impeachment by other members of the group. The moderator tries to stifle dissent by completely censoring the rebel's postings, and the flames spill into unmoderated newsgroups and e-mail. Anyone familiar with revolutionary history knows what comes next: a splinter newsgroup is formed, opposition builds, and the moderator becomes more dogmatic, more repressive, in an attempt to prevent further disaffection. But it's too late—whipped up by a small group of antimoderates, freed from restrictive netiquette, the great mob rises up against its leader and either dethrones or deserts him. The defeated moderator slinks off to some ex-moderator chat room to commiserate with other ousted leaders. The newsgroup, with a new moderator in place, begins the cycle again.

All this just to talk about cornstarch recipes.

Gopher, FTP, WAIS, and All That Other Useless Stuff

You don't want to have anything to do with this stuff, because most of it is practical, and you don't want that—you want bells and whistles, roll-overs and audio, blinking letters and animations. The people who use this stuff are concerned only with getting on the Net, downloading the information they require, and getting off the Net to make use of that information. Boring! That's not what the Net is about. Anyway, here's a little guide to the stuff you'll never use.

Gopher is a transfer protocol, developed and supported by the University of Minnesota, for retrieving data from the Internet. Its name comes from the program's ability to "go for" needed information, which is what passes for clever at the University of Minnesota. Using Gopher is discouraged these days, since it doesn't keep you online very long; some on-line services don't even give you the option of using it. America Online keeps its customers away from Gopher by using a scary, buck-toothed rodent in a hole as an icon.

FTP stands for "File Transfer Protocol," three words that make sense to you separately but confuse you utterly when used together. Developed early in the 1960s, this is simply an efficient and inexpensive fuel additive that guarantees increased engine performance. In fact, many professional race car drivers use it to . . . hold it, that's *STP*. Then what the hell is FTP?

Oh, yeah. FTP is just one method dedicated to transferring files from one Internet-linked computer to another. If you connect to another computer via FTP, you access the remote computer's public directory—the one that stores all the files that any Net surfer can download and play with. Depending on your communications software, you'll see some version of the following:

```
CONNECTED VIA FTP TO /PUB OF FRITZ WEAVER UNIVERSITY

/pub                   date      size

..parent directory
readme.txt             1/01/81   645
```

```
vaughn.jpg          9/19/92     23408
vaughn.txt          9/19/92     310
christie.jpg        7/14/94     32116
christie.txt        7/14/94     305
dseed.txt           8/01/95     2114
dseed.scr           10/10/95    310725
daniels.jpg         02/10/96    44210
daniels.txt         02/10/96    440
hasselhoff.jpg      02/10/96    56120
hasselhoff.txt      02/10/96    127
mulhare.jpg         02/10/96    33540
mulhare.txt         02/10/96    205
kitt.scr            02/10/96    130004
dehaven.jpg         03/17/96    23684
dehaven.txt         03/17/96    330
jvandyke.jpg        03/17/96    64312
jvandyke.txt        03/17/96    175
momcar.scr          03/17/96    156783
```

This is a directory listing similar to that on your own computer. And just like your own computer, you haven't the faintest idea what all these files are. You know that .txt means "text," and you have a vague idea that a .jpg file is a picture file, but you can't be sure. Where do you turn for information? Try the readme.txt file. Some communications software lets you open up and view the file without downloading it—by double-clicking on the filename, or choosing "view file" from an onscreen menu. If you can manage to open up the file, you find a treasure trove of information:

CONTENTS OF /PUB/README.TXT:

Eines Morgens erwachte Gregor Samsa aus unruhigen Träumen und fand sich in seinem Bett zu einem ungeheueren Ungeziefer verwandelt.

This illustrates one of the drawbacks of FTP: unless a file on the remote computer tells you what you've gotten yourself into, you'll have a hard time discovering just what this particular computer is offering you. In fact, this particular directory is dedicated to movies and television shows that feature famous actors portraying inanimate objects. You can download pictures, reviews, and scripts from the movie *Demon Seed*, and the TV shows "Knight Rider" and "My Mother, the Car."

WAIS stands for "Quick Search of Internet Databases." This should, by all rights, spell not WAIS but QSID. But the guy who invented it started typing with his fingers one letter off of his home keys, so WAIS it is.

IRC stands for "Internet Relay Chat," a method of carrying on real-time conversation on the Internet. Like CompuServe's CB or AOL's Chat Room services, IRC is broken up into separate "channels," each devoted to a particular topic. Although IRC has been around since the late 1980s (it was put together by some jerko from Finland), it has already developed a mystifying code of conduct that put bushido to shame. Adopting the same policy that made the Shaker religion so enduring, IRC buffs refuse to help, welcome, talk to, recognize, or tolerate "newbies." In order to discourage new blood, these same IRChatters insist on using inelegant software, clumsy syntax, and incomprehensible acronyms. To further discourage anyone new from bothering them, IRC buffs give their channels misleading names—the "Picket Fences" channel has nothing to do with the television show.

Internet Cafes: Where Communication and Cuisine Collide

What's the first thing you think of when someone says "hacker"? Good food, right? What could be more natural than the combination of delicate electronic equipment and crumbs? The birth of the Internet-based eatery can be traced to a chance encounter at the corner of 23rd Street and Fifth Avenue in New York City. Two men were rushing through the morning rain: one, a deli owner delivering coffee to a nearby FedEx office; the other, a computer technician returning a refurbished Macintosh to a neighborhood company. The two collided, inspiring the now famous exchange:

"Hey! You got coffee on my computer!"

"Well, you dropped your computer on my coffee!"

Two weeks later the first digital deli opened. Soon similar establishments were sprouting throughout the country. The competition for most cloying name was fierce, what with entrants like A Byte to Eat, RAM 'n' Ramen, eat@Joe's, and Chewy GUI and Good; perhaps the stupidest name belonged to Chicago's short-lived International House of Flamed Spam.

Whatever the name, the setup at each of these places follows one of two templates: the grunge model and the Barnes & Noble model.

Grunge Template

Grunge Internet cafes, rather than attempting to make the Info-bahn accessible to us commoners, try to make us commoners into the kind of geeks who have been surfing on-line for years. To that end, the cafes are constructed to provide maximum Internet access, minimal light, minimal instruction, minimal food and service, and maximal safety code violations. Computers—that is to say, motherboards without covers—are haphazardly shoved underneath tables scattered throughout a dark pit. The one guy who actually knows anything about the place's antediluvian computers is always "on his way back" from some distant land. Needless to say, he never shows up, no matter how long you stay. Your only company (besides the short-order cook in the back) is a disinterested bartender/waitress/cashier/receptionist/bus boy/manager who, rather than attempt to juggle all her duties, has turned her back to everyone and is trying to move the speed rack with her thought waves.

The Barnes & Noble Template

The other kind of Internet cafe tries to make its operation a digital home for consumers. Here, color-coordinated waiters provide timely and helpful assistance, eager to supply browser training or oversized muffins with overrated coffees. The machines work remarkably well. T-1 lines make linking between Web sites a joy to watch. Suddenly, it's easy to see what all the Internet fuss is about!

Which type of cafe should you patronize? The grunge cafe, of course. Spend a few hours at a cafe with good equipment and service, and you'll go home to your rotten little computer hating it, your job, and your life. Hang out at the grunge cafe, and you'll be eager to go home to your cute little computer.

Chapter 12

The World Wide Web

Once upon a time, the CD-ROM was the Grand Savior of All Civilization. That title has now been bestowed upon the World Wide Web. Ironically, it was a CD-ROM that led to the Web's preeminence in cyberspace. The CD-ROM game *MYST* proved that people would spend hours wandering around some virtual world, getting absolutely nothing accomplished, so long as there were pretty graphics involved. This was the inspiration for the World Wide Web, which combines hours of useless graphics-mongering with usurious telephone connect charges. Nowhere is the Web's preeminence in cyberspace better seen than in the sudden proliferation of Web designers, firms that construct Websites for other businesses. These new entrepreneurs have a lot in common with those who jumped into the CD-ROM field to make their fortunes. In fact, they're the same guys—having been blown out of the CD-ROM business, they're now looking to make a few million designing Web pages for other businesses. Within a couple of years, most of them will be unemployed again, looking for the next opportunity to lose their shirts.

The World Wide Web is the most comprehensive format for accessing the Internet to date. It not only offers a more interesting and entertaining interface for taking advantage of information on the Net, it encompasses older, more restrictive interfaces. Good Web browsers can make FTP transfers, conduct Gopher and WAIS searches, access newsgroups, and handle electronic mail as well.

The building block of the World Wide Web is the Web page, which is simply another format for presenting resources available on the Internet. Unlike other formats, Web pages have interactive multimedia capability, which boils down to the fact that you can now take the *Cosmo* Sex Quiz without a pencil.

The Web essentially breaks down into two forms: commercial and personal advertisements. You've got your corporate Web pages, like the Fox Network home page, where you can wait twenty minutes to load a fuzzy graphic of a show that you don't watch; and you've got your private Web pages, where you can wait five minutes to load a page that some troubled loner has dedicated to "The Glory That Is Fess Parker." That's about it, too. Oh, there are links that will take you from that Fox Network home page to a private page celebrating the extinct "Alien Nation" show, and links taking you from the Fess Parker home page to the alt.fan.ed.ames newsgroup, but they're all just variations on a theme. And the hype is so pervasive, the need to discover the latest in technology so powerful, that few people notice what the World Wide Web is really about: keeping you on-line long enough to bankrupt you.

What's a Webmaster?

A Webmaster is the guy in charge of a particular Web page. There is no Webmaster's degree or Webmaster school; you get to call yourself a Webmaster just by putting out a Web page, no matter how junky it is. Come to think of it, you can call yourself a Webmaster even if you don't have a Web page. You can call yourself anything you want, really. This is just to warn you against contacting

any old Webmaster for assistance. There are good Webmasters, and there are evil Webmasters.

A Few Web Terms

The URL (Universal Resource Locator) is a means of identifying the location of the Web page to which you have linked. You generally won't have to type this kind of clumsy address—you'll be linking from other pages, and as you go from page to page your browser will automatically update the URL for you. It's a good idea to glance at the URL from time to time, though. Say you're looking for steps to take in the event of swallowing some household poison, and you link to the "What to Do If You Swallow Poison" page. If the URL has

A Sample Web Page

If you've seen one personal Web page, you've seen them all. Here's one.

Nils Schmenken's Home Page

Hi! Welcome to my page! Who am I? I'm Nils Schmenken, a Danish exchange student in my third year at AAMCO Tech. I am majoring in Philosophy and Transmission Rebuild, but I have plenty of spare time for my real interests:

Here's my page honoring the best actor in the world, John Stamos . . . :)
. . . and one for the best actress in the world, Hildegarde Knef. :)

I hate Lent, but I sure love höckepöckes!
What's a höckepöcke? It's a delectable Danish pastry baked at the end of every Lenten period, made with elderberries, apricot brandy, and dirt. Here's the recipe!

Some relly cool links . . .

Eddie Prochter's <u>Claudia Schiffer</u> page (lots of pics)
Claudia Schiffer's <u>Eddie Prochter</u> page (lots of lawsuits)
My friend Max Nielsen's shrine to <u>Pneumatic Actuators</u>

Search Engines . . .

Yahoo
Webcrawler
Yeeha

comments? questions? feedback? anything? please e-mail me, I'm so lonely.
I even took my counter off because it was so depressing, just staring at the
00000 every day. talk to me. please.
<u>nschmenken@aamco.edu</u>

---

some reputable medical authority associated with it, you're okay.
But if the URL reads:

http://www.attica.deathrow/serial__killer/personal.html

the medical advice is probably suspect.

HTML (HyperText Mark-up Language) is the programming language
that formats Web pages, allowing them to make use of links, graphics,
animations, input forms, and the like. HTML is relatively easy to master, which means that almost anyone can construct a reasonable-
looking Web page—even you! The bad news is, of course, that your
idiot neighbor can also have his own Web page.

Remember FTP? That was the protocol for transferring files between computers on the Net (including yours). Well, HTTP
(HyperText Transfer Protocol) is the protocol for transferring
HyperText between computers on the Net. Is this getting any
clearer, or do you give up? I give up too.

HST (Harry S Truman), thirty-third president of the United States, made the decision to drop the atomic bomb over Hiroshima. If only he had dropped it on Carrot Top instead.

The Browser

The browser is your link to the Web, and its usefulness is best expressed in its name. This handy software package isn't a Web finder or helper or extractor or anything that promises you will ever get something accomplished. This is a browser, taken from the verb "to browse," which is what you're used to doing at the nearest mall—wandering around aimlessly, looking at junk you're never going to buy, eat, or play, until your back starts to ache and all you want to do is lie down and die. The Web browser brings that same experience to the Internet.

There are quite a few browsers out there—NCSA Mosaic, Microsoft, Win- and MacWeb, for example—and one monster browser, Netscape Navigator. Netscape is the brainchild of Marc Andreessen—whose name is actually Anderson but, being a techie kind of guy, naturally he can't spell it. Netscape is to Web browsers what Microsoft is to PCs: an energetic, ambitious, young company whose capabilities are just a few months behind its promises.

Browser Features

Certain features are shared by all browsers. The most interesting of these is the Browser logo, which usually sits somewhere in the upper right or left hand corner of the browser screen. Whenever you're waiting to load a Web page, the logo does something it thinks is amusing—spinning, flashing, or animating in some fashion. This waste of memory is supposed to keep you from glancing at your watch and noticing how long this is taking, but it only works on people who are fascinated by other monotonous displays—a spinning dryer, a Yule log, or the current season of "Saturday Night Live."

Here are some common browser commands, and what they mean:

Back   Take me back to the page I left, because although I hated that page, at least it loaded quickly.

Forward   I forgot how much I hated this page. Let's see if the next one loads this time.

Reload   Maybe if I double-click just right the page will load properly.

Stop   There have been "five seconds remaining" for the last half hour. I quit.

Exit   Why is this the only command that does what I want it to?

Browser Caches

One of the most obvious features of a Web page is its ability to display graphics. From little round, multi-colored buttons to half-page graphics files, every Web page has its own unique combination of graphics. What many people don't know is that your browser takes every single one of these little graphics files, and sticks it on your hard drive. Your browser directory has a subdirectory called CACHE, which is one of those words you like to stay away from in any situation. This is where all those little graphics files go. Why does your browser do this? If you ever decide to return to a particular page, the browser won't have to download the graphics file in order to display it—it can simply pull it up from that CACHE subdirectory. And since loading something off the hard drive is faster than getting it off the Net, you'll be able to load that page faster.

All of this will mean very little to you until the day you discover you have no more free space on your hard disk, because your browser has saved a trillion of those tiny little files in that CACHE subdirectory. When this happens, you should immediately purge your cache of these ant-like files. Load your browser, head for the "Purge Cache Now" button, and click on it. Now slowly walk to the nearest Walmart and back. By the time you return, most of the files will have been deleted.

Bookmarks

Browsers give you the ability to keep a list of your favorite Web sites, by using what it likes to call "bookmarks." Whenever you land on a site you want to remember, you don't have to write down the URL, you just have to bookmark the site. As a rule, after your first three days of Web browsing you will have collected about seven hundred and fifty bookmarks; thereafter you will begin scaling back, deleting bookmarks, until you're left with a list that contains three search engines and your high school reunion page.

Forums on the Web

Many Web pages have newsgroup-like forums that allow visitors to use the best information resource on the Net: people. Memberships

in such forums are restricted to specific Web pages, so you don't
get the same amount of junk that you see with Usenet newsgroups.

A sample transcript of someone looking for a Cole Porter lyric,
posted to the "Gettin' A Kick" Web page devoted to Cole Porter:

```
7/14/96
to: anyone
from: annie.a__nun@anon.nana
re: COFFEE SONG
   HELP! CAN ANYONE TELL ME IF COLE PORTER WROTE THE SONG ABOUT
   COFFEE IN BRAZIL?
   THANX!


7/19/96
to: annie.a__nun@anon.nana
from: jiggscasey@ecom.con
re: coffee song
   why are you shouting?


7/20/96
to: annie.a__nun@anon.nana
from: d__mathews@cut.cut.cut.com
re: coffee song
   It was Porter Wagonner.


7/20/96
to: annie.a__nun@anon.nana
from: lamarr@brooks.mel
re: Coffee Song
   It was Lyle Wagonner.


7/22/96
to: annie.a__nun@anon.nana
from: Q.T.Pi@aol.com
re: Coffee Song
   me too
```

```
7/22/96
to: annie.a__nun@anon.nana
from: doolittle@allo.gov
re: Coffee Song
   IMHO it was ABBA.
   Or maybe vice versa.

7/24/96
to: annie.a__nun@anon.nana
from: pres@tetley.com
re: Coffee Song
   ``Tea for Two'' is a better song.
   I think Vincent Youmans wrote it.
   ``Tea for Two'' that is.

7/26/96
to: annie.a__nun@anon.nana
from: blathering-idiot@liberty.com
re: Coffee Song
   I know Cole Porter wrote a bunch of songs for an AIDS
   fundraising record. Why don't you just write him and
   ask?

7/27/95
to: everyone
from: annie.a__nun@anon.nana
re: COFFEE SONG
   THANKS FOR ALL YOUR HELP! NOT JUST THE PEOPLE WHO POSTED HERE IN
   THE FORUM, BUT THOSE WHO SENT ME E-MAIL, SNAIL MAIL, CALLED ME ON
   THE PHONE, AND EVEN DROPPED BY MY HOUSE TO OFFER SUGGESTIONS! I
   HAVE NEVER EXPERIENCED SUCH AN OUTPOURING OF COMMUNITY CONCERN!
   MAY YOU ALL ROT IN HELL!
```

Mailing Lists

Web pages offer visitors the chance to sign up for mailing lists dedicated to their particular interests. If you sign up for any of them,
you can expect between three and four hundred thousand inane

messages in your mailbox every day, as well as a note from your provider to close your account and go away.

Security on the Web

There is a lot of concern about the security of Internet transactions. Many people are wary of shopping on the Net, lest some unsavory hacker discover their credit card number. Of course, these are the same people who hand their American Express cards to paroled forgers working as grocery delivery boys, but we'll let that pass.

Exploring the Web

The glory of the World Wide Web is the freedom it allows you to just bop from place to place, clicking on links that look interesting or useful and checking out commercial goods, free software, personal pages, interest groups, and recent e-mail. As any Web veteran

The Password Is . . .

Are you sick of stockpiling passwords and user names yet? A year ago, all you had to remember was your calling card number, ATM code, and maybe the password to an on-line service or local BBS. Now every other Web page asks you to register with them and pick a password. Of course you rarely use the same password, because for some reason you don't want one imprudent keyboard entry in the presence of an erstwhile friend to unlock the entirety of your life. Lord knows you wouldn't want someone posing as you to wreck your standing at the Marie Osmond home page, the Fig-Lovers home page, and the Virtual Velveeta Kitchen. But how can you possibly keep track of all your passwords?

Easy—just jot them all down in any word processing file on your computer, and give the files one of the following names:

readme.txt
order.frm
register.doc

No one will ever see them.

can tell you, Web pages link you to other Web pages, each of which either has almost what you're looking for, or offers tantalizing clues to a site where you might find what you're looking for. You never will find what you're looking for, of course; the essence of the Web is the digital mirages of your goal that it always offers. And no matter how many times you've cursed in frustration and sworn that you've given up the Web forever, you'll eventually come back, hoping that they (whoever they are) have finally "fixed" the Web so you can make good use of it.

It ain't gonna happen.

Search Engines

The search engine is an invaluable tool for getting around the Web with your sanity intact. A search engine relies on user-supplied keywords to produce a list of available Web resources about those keywords.

For instance, if you want to dig up a specific piece of information about Led Zeppelin legend Jimmy Page, you can just enter "Page" in the little input box, hit "search," and wait. After about twenty-seven hours you'll get a listing of six billion Web sites, and realize that "Page" is a little too broad a search term, considering that almost everything on the Web is a page. Laughing at your own folly, a little wiser now, you initiate another search, this time using "Jimmy Page." A mere nine hours later you get a list of about thirty thousand sites that includes Jimmy Buffet's Page, as well as Jimmy Troiani's Patti Page Page. Only now realizing just how restrictive you need to make your search, you enter "Page" and "Jimmy" and "Led" and "Zeppelin." After five minutes the results of your query appear:

> RESULTS OF "JIMMY" + "PAGE" + "LED" + "ZEPPELIN":
> *The Official Led Zeppelin Page*
> *The Unofficial Led Zeppelin Page*
> *The Web Shrine to the Greatest Guitarist in the Universe*
> *Stairway to Jimmy*
> *Seven Reasons to Hate Led Zeppelin*
> *The Lakehurst Dispatch, Vol. XII, Number 7 May 1937*
> *Jimmy Page Rules!*
> *The Jimmy Page Songbook*

Your initial elation turns to despair as you click on each link, only to find the same thing awaits you:

BAD URL.
Update your links, for Christ's sake, will ya?

(Okay, maybe not the same thing every time. Sometimes you get that Forbidden Server message that makes you think you've broken a law.) The only link that works is the *Lakehurst Dispatch* of 1937, which connects you to the following:

> "... the Hindenburg's second cook, Gerhart Bruckner, was blinded by the thick smoke. Fortunately, 11-year-old passenger Jimmy Ross, taking a page from Tom Mix, threw a rope around Bruckner and led him from the burning zeppelin."

After hours of fruitless effort, you're glad to finally have a piece of concrete information, even if it isn't what you set out for. You don't remember what you wanted to know about Jimmy Page, anyway.

Hot Lists

In addition to the considerable number of search engines at your disposal, there are numerous Web sites that rate other Web sites according to how hot, cool, lame, crass, or useless they are. It's only a matter of time before someone comes up with the brilliant idea of an annual Web Page Award Show, simulcast both on television and on the Internet. The name of the award itself will be determined by popular e-mail vote, and the voting will break down along the following lines:

The Webby	34%
The Urly	27%
The Yahooey	19%
The Golden Link	11%
The HTTP://WWW%AW	7%
The TCP/IP Freely Memorial Award	1.99%
Ron	.001%

It's certainly fun to have all these hot lists around, but it's not really what we need. What is a hot list anyway? It's either a list of what one person thinks is cool, or what a billion people think is cool. Your chances of liking the same things as some pathetic loner who needs to alert the rest of the world to his favorite places are pretty slim—as are your chances of linking to a site that a billion other people are clamoring to get on. Hot lists aren't what we need. What we need are arbitration engines.

Arbitration Engines

Instead of thinking of Web pages as pages, think of them as individual television channels. You've got your major programs, like Time's Pathfinder site, and your public access programs, like Nils Schmenken's Home Page. Except with the Web there's no limit to the number of channels. Think about that for a moment. Most of the country has only 100 television channels or less, and already there's not enough content to go around. Original programming only makes up about 3 percent of what goes on the air; the rest is repackaging—shows like "Before They Were Stars," "TV's Greatest Commercials," and "TV's Greatest 'Before They Were Stars' Shows." The Web, on the other hand, already has millions of little television stations, called Web sites and Web pages, with no end in sight. What kind of content can possibly fill up all that dead space?

Everything, that's what. Everything anyone can think of will one day be on the Web, from fact to fiction to speculation to opinion to deception. Actually, since it's a lot easier to make up stuff than to discover the truth, there will be a greater number of lies on the Web than there are truths. What's more, there won't be any way to distinguish between honest and deceptive sites—after all, with HTML anyone can put together a reasonable-looking Web page. Take a couple of keywords, like "physics" and "quantum," plug them into a search engine like Alta Vista, and look over the list that pops up. Nestled among the stuff from Cal Tech, Brookhaven, and CERN, is an interesting document from the East Stroudsburg Research Institute for Quantum Research. Since you once got stuck in East Stroudsburg for an interminable afternoon, you click on that document and behold! There are the results of a study proving that protons decay under the influence of human alpha waves! If you didn't know any better, you might actually believe this malarkey.

In a few years, there will be ten times more of that kind of nonsense on the Web than there is true stuff. Why? For one thing, more people lie than tell the truth. For another, it takes a lot longer to accurately describe the physical apparatus used in a scientific experiment than to say "Hey—I bent a key with my mind!"

This information parity will give rise to arbitration engines. Arbitration engines, staffed by eminent experts in various fields, will publish lists of sites they have deemed either reputable or bogus. Different engines will have different focuses and panels, but they will all want James Randi as a member. (And, of course, about a week after the first arbitration engine is established, the first fake arbitration engine will appear.) Their lists will discourage people from frequenting sites like:

The World Wide Web Official Interactive Shell Game

The You May Already Have Won 100,000 Cyberdollars Page

The Illegal Immigrant Lottery Winners' Home Page

Your Quantum Psychic

The New York Times

Cowboys and Engines

Just kidding.

Using the Web

I know what you're thinking: Thanks for all the info, pal, but exactly how do I go about making use of this World Wide Web thing? What is there to actually do there? How can I get the most out of the Web? And while you're at it, what's all this about a flat tax?

There's almost no end to the number of ways the Web can make day-to-day living more interesting, more resourceful, and more sedentary. In this section we'll talk about the wonderful utility and versatility of the Web. Here's just a sampling of the kinds of things you can do, and an example or two of the kind of page you can visit for each activity.

Retrieve Information

Retrieving information on the Web, with its myriad libraries, file servers, on-line experts, schools and universities, forums, and discussion groups, is a snap. Retrieving information that you're actually looking for is another matter. You know what it's like whenever you go to the video store to pick up a tape, spend six hours trying to decide what to rent, and finally come up with the one title they don't have in stock? It's the same on the Web.

Example:

The Stupid TV Detective Gimmick Database (www.hook.com). Lists all the gimmicks used by creators of television detectives. Links to Overeaters' Anonymous, The Braille Society, Hair Club for Men, etc.

175

Working Hard?

The absolute worst times to try to get on the Web are around 9 in the morning and 5 in the evening. No, this isn't because everyone logs on just before going to work and just after getting home; it's because everyone logs on just *after* getting to work and *before* leaving for home. Why pay for multi-player Duke Nukem yourself by logging in from your home, when your boss can foot the bill? A lot of employees actually arrive an hour or so before they have to be working and stay late in the evening just to check out the latest cool Websites. Some manage to advertise the long hours they put in while hiding their actual activity, so they acquire reputations as hard workers; the cleverest of them even manage to get paid overtime. One legendary civil servant managed to rack up enough overtime to buy a summer home in Easthampton, then turned around and sued the government for disability, based on a complaint called "Netscabies."

Shop

This is what's it's all about, really—getting you to shop on the Web. This is the Holy Grail of Internet Capitalism. It's what the heads of companies like Sears, Blockbuster Video, and Sam Goody dream of when they're tucked away every night: an entire country of desk-bound consumers, double-clicking to order goods without ever leaving the house. No more retail outlets, no more employees, no more customer complaint windows, no more ex-con rent-a-cops dozing off by the front door, no more maintenance workers partying at night instead of waxing the floors, no more lawsuits about the uneven sidewalk in front of the store, no more neighborhood protests over the opening—or closing—of a retail superstore. Instead, just one manufacturing and shipping plant the size of Rhode Island, built in a right-to-work Sun Belt state, with just one enormous machine to take orders from the company Website, operate the automated merchandise packager, and notify the shipper to pick up packages from an automatic, conveyer belt–equipped loading dock.

Now you know why so many commercial Websites want to send you little gifts for registering—a mouse pad here, a clock radio there. They want you to relax and grow accustomed to getting neat stuff over the Web. That way, you'll tell your friends, and they'll visit commercial sites too, to get some free stuff. Pretty soon, everyone will be feeling pretty good about having things delivered to them via the Web. It'll be so much fun that the transition from getting free stuff to getting ripped off will be all but undetectable.

Example:

The Galloping Green Grocer (www.victual.reality.com). Yes, now you can even order groceries on-line! Have them picked out, bagged, and delivered right to your door—where you have to do an immediate inventory to see how much spoiled fruit you've gotten, and how much stuff the delivery man has eaten on the way over!

Make New Friends

It's easy to make new friends on the Web. Every private Web page has an e-mail link, where you can leave messages for the guy whose page it is. And let's face it: there's nobody needier than someone who has his own Web page. If he's not looking for a friend, he's looking for a mate; if he's not looking for a mate, he's looking for a job; if he's not looking for a job, he's looking for someone as miserable as he. Anyway you slice it, he's needy. If you leave e-mail at every private Web page you visit, you'll have friends within the hour. Some of these guys are just sitting there waiting for their in-box bell to ring.

Example:

Nils Schmenken's Home Page (www.aamco.edu/users/losers/nschmenken). He's been waiting a long time. (Warning: Don't eat the höckepöckes.)

Meet Your Mate!

In addition to needy Web page owners, there are plenty of needy single people out there making cautious forays into the world of cyberdating. Cyberdating has a huge base of potential clients, so the odds of meeting someone compatible are greatly increased by making use of the Web. The hardest part is trying to convince yourself that, somehow, a Web browser and 28.8 bps modem have made you less of a loser than before.

Example:

Cher and Cher Alike (www.ex-toy.com). This page keeps a comprehensive list of Cher's ex-boyfriends. The list supplies e-mail addresses of her rejected suitors and is updated almost daily.

Next!! (www.may-december.com). This Website gives all pertinent information for anyone who wishes to become Cher's next boyfriend.

Contact the Federal Authorities!

The way you're leaving messages and making dates all over the Web, odds are you're going to run into some pretty strange cyberneighbors. If your attempts to ignore them are of no avail, and you keep getting threatening e-mail with attached bitmaps of Jonestown, you can stop by the FBI Web page! Drop them a note.

Example:

The Federal Bureau of Investigation (www.fedz.gov). Note: Don't be confused by the "Message from the Director." FBI Director Louis J. Freeh has legally changed his name to World B. Freeh.

Have Some Plain Old Fun

There's a cute game called "History" that can make any Web session a barrel o' laughs. Let's say you logged on in order to find out how your congressional representative voted on the telecommunications bill; now it's three hours later and you're staring at the lyrics to Michael Nesmith's song "Joanne." Instead of just saving the lyrics (of course you're going to save them—you've always wanted to know the words to "Joanne") and logging off, try answering the rhetorical question that comes at the end of every Web session— "Now how the hell did I get here?" Take a pen and paper (or risk crashing your computer by opening up a notebook application), and jot down the various steps that led you to your present Website. Then check them against the "History" feature of your browser (look for it, it's there). Here's how you score:

- At least 75 percent of the steps right: you get to disconnect immediately and watch "Law and Order"

- 50-75 percent right: you have to browse until you see the words "Netscape enhanced"

- 25-50 percent right: you have to browse until you see the words "Really cool links"

- 10-25 percent right: you have to browse until you see the words "good Gin Blossoms song"

- Less than 10 percent right: you have to browse until you see the words "Exxon rules"

Find Long-Lost Friends

Did you ever wonder what happened to that old high school sweetheart of yours? Using the many resources of the Web—phone books, high school alumni pages, faraway friends on-line—you have a great chance of staging a Web Reunion. Just watch out your old flame doesn't stop by the FBI Web page and complain about you.

Example:

Remember Me? (www.revenge.com). You supply the name of the girl/boy who broke your heart in ninth grade by referring to your short pants as culottes. If she/he has an e-mail address, the boys at Remember Me? will make sure she/he receives a note from a fictional high school classmate, raving about you and your choice of the following: Nobel prize, sexual prowess, wealth, buddy Brad Pitt/ Jennifer Aniston/Elton John, mansion, Brady Bunch lunchbox.

Pretend You're Someone Else

It's a matter of fact that 73 percent of the world's people wish they were someone else. Another 26 percent are happy with themselves, but wish their circumstances were different. The remaining 1 percent are happy with themselves and content with their circumstances, and if they know what's good for them they'll continue to keep their mouths shut.

Until real-time videoconferencing has become a reality, personal computing in general, and the Internet in particular, gives you the opportunity to be something you're not—rich, poor, smart, dense, attractive, successful, down-on-your-luck, whatever. Whether playing a game of computer baccarat with the future of mankind at stake, or visiting an on-line chat room as J.D. Salinger, you never have to settle for just being yourself. Becoming another person is as simple as choosing a new user name.

This kind of thing is more commonplace than you might think. A major on-line service recently did a confidential poll concerning their chat rooms, and made the following discoveries:

- Of the twenty-five members in the "Lesbian Chat" room, twenty-four were teenage boys.

- Not one adult member of the "Impeach Clinton" room had ever voted.

- Fourteen people in the "Lollapalooza" room claimed to be Courtney Love.

- Of the fifty people in the "Justice for O.J." room, forty-eight were actually O.J. Simpson, one was Robert Kardashian, and one was someone claiming to be Courtney Love.

Example:

Megan Kot's Page (www.books.org). *Your* name is Asher Lev.

Control Things at a Distance

Some of the most popular Websites are those equipped to let you manipulate some local object, the most obvious example being a page that lets you run a model train in Germany. (Running it on time, however, is considered in bad taste.) An on-site camera lets you view the action. You get all the fun of manipulating something at a distance, and so does the guy who manipulated you into doing it.

Find Dirty Stuff

Q. What's the first thing Web newcomers want to know?

A. "Where's all the dirty stuff?"

Of course, not everyone asks the question that way. Some people actually try something like "You know something? I'd like to see what all the commotion regarding prurient material on the Internet is about," as if they're just concerned citizens researching a constitutional dispute. However they phrase it, their real goal is to make sure they get to see some of that dirty stuff before it gets censored. That pesky telecommunications bill threatens to shut down naughty Web pages just as it does newsgroups.

When the 1996 passage of the telecommunications bill signaled an unprecedented assault on freedom, free speech defenders protested by turning the backgrounds of their Web pages black the day the telecommunications bill was signed—a bold move that demonstrated just how much better Web pages look with black backgrounds. But these freedom fighters weren't done yet—no, they knew that in order to convince the country of the seriousness of the threat, they had to adopt an official protest ribbon. Soon, blue ribbons began popping up on sites throughout the Web. Unfortunately, seeing as how the blue ribbon is a traditional sign not of protest but excellence, most people thought the ribbons were some sort of award for Web design, like the Urly or the Ron.

You might well ask: What's all the fuss about, anyway? Dirty stuff has been available in magazines, videotapes, books, comics, stage shows, bus advertisements, television programs, Olympic ice dancing, playing cards, and Pep Boys' matchbooks for years now. Why the outrage over its appearance in cyberspace? Aren't there more pressing problems for people to be concerned with—crime, poverty, injustice, random violence, natural disaster, and death?

Well, no. You've got it backwards. Crime, poverty, injustice, random violence, natural disaster, and death are only *symptoms* of a greater problem: dirty stuff on the Internet. Once we get rid of all the dirty stuff, all those symptoms will disappear. Of course, once we get rid of all the dirty stuff on the Internet, the Internet itself will disappear.

Example:

The Aromatherapy Home Page (www.stink.net). Talk about obscene.

Contact Your Representatives

For too many years, getting in touch with your elected representatives was a tortuous process. First, you had to remember just who they were. Then you had to figure out how to express your feelings in a manner that wouldn't attract the attention of the federal authorities. And then, worst of all, you had to find a stamp.

No longer. Nowadays, there are Web pages that can tell you the names of your representatives, and provide you with appropriate pre-written e-mail letters to send. All you have to do is select the representative and the topic, and then choose the attitude you wish to convey: Disappointed, Aggravated, or Disgusted. Still other Websites allow you to petition elected officials for services to the constituency.

Example:

Corn 'R' Us (www.agro.gov). You can apply for your own farm subsidy at this Website. A word of caution, though: there are the usual stringent rules for qualification, like knowing how to spell *milk*.

I Have Seen the Future of the Web and It Looks Like Bad Public Access Television

Since it looks like the Web is here to stay, a lot of fun stuff is being developed to make it even more interactive, entertaining, and expensive. The good news is that these Web innovations don't have clumsy, inaccessible names like HTML and TCP/IP. The bad news is that they have cloying names like Java, Shockwave, and Afterburn. And the usual news is that you're two upgrades away from using any of it. Here's a brief rundown of some of these developments:

Shockwave gives you the ability to run animations on the Web that have been created using a program known as Director, from Macromedia. For instance, if you want to shop for a new Ford 350 pick-up these days, their Website gives you the opportunity to look at your favorite model in a number of colors. But with Shockwave, you'll be able to see something a little more relevant: an animation demonstrating that this year's model doesn't explode when broadsided by another vehicle.

RealAudio is a process that allows you to play real-time audio off of the Internet, and is already in use by many Web sites. With the RealAudio application installed on your computer, you can listen to

NPR programs, live classical performances, interviews, and news of the day. The only remaining problem to be solved is how to turn your radio into a computer.

Sun Microsystems's Java programming language creates applets. No, applets aren't those things on your shoelaces. They are miniature applications. When you load a Java-designed Web page into your computer's memory, you don't just download the text and graphics. You also load an applet that runs on your computer—for instance, a page using Java might allow you to enter your present income and future needs, and calculate how nasty your "Golden Years" are going to be.

Klemperer Incorporated's Coma language makes use of the same technology that enables a DataLink wristwatch to receive data from your monitor screen. When you load a Website using Coma, little beams of infrared light are emitted from your monitor at a hypnotic frequency, placing you in a trance-like state. When the Web page is completely loaded, the beams stop. Not only do you awaken feeling refreshed, but it seems to you as though the page has loaded instantly! (Note: Beta versions of Coma, available for public downloading from the Klemperer Website, should not be tested by the following: epileptics, narcoleptics, schizophrenics, pregnant women, crack addicts, professional wrestlers, dental hygienists, or John Tesh.)

VRML Plug-ins will enable 3-D viewing of Web objects and animations, once developers work out a small glitch in this groundbreaking product. The glitch? Nobody cares.

Chapter 13

The Future

Many people ask: "What's the future going to look like?" as if they had already figured out the past and the present. Rather than respond with a Doris Day song, I will hazard a few guesses about the far-reaching changes that the Digital Revolution will bring.

Ignorance Will Go Through the Roof

Contrary to cyberpundits' prediction that ignorance will diminish as the Internet begins flooding American households with rich new sources of information, just the opposite will occur. Accessibility to the Internet only guarantees that there will be thousands more news sources for the public to ignore.

After all, even today there are countless newspapers, magazines, television programs, radio shows, books, tapes, and CDs available to us. And what are America's main sources of information? The front page of *USA Today*, Tabitha Soren's periodic klatsches with bemused political figures, Howard Stern's daily radio broadcast, and however much of the 11 o'clock local news you unintentionally see before switching to a syndicated rerun of "Seinfeld."

There Will Be No Real-Time Electronic Conversation

Right now, technicians are working feverishly to perfect real-time voice/video transmission between computers. What does this mean? It means that within the next few years, all long distance communications will be audiovisual. At that point, real-time conversation will cease almost completely. Let's face it: how many times would you answer your phone if you knew that the caller would be able to see you?

Here's the scenario of the future: It's eleven o'clock in the morning. You're at home, supposedly working on a proposal due next Wednesday, but what you're really up to is watching an infomercial about car wax. Your computer beeps, or quacks, or does whatever you've told it to do whenever there's a call; from your memory-resident caller ID application, you see that it's a call from your supervisor. What are you going to do—push <Enter> to pick up the computer videophone, and let the boss see you standing there in your robe with the television on in the background? Nope. Nor are you going to block video transmission and simply answer the audio, because that just looks suspicious. You let the answering software pick up. While your supervisor leaves a message, you quickly dress, squelch the television, and spread some work out around the computer. Then you stick a pencil in your mouth and call back, explaining to your supervisor that you were just in the bathroom.

"That's odd," says your supervisor. "I must be psychic."

"Why is that?"

"Because every single time I call you, you're in the bathroom. As a matter of fact, every single time I call any one of my employees, he or she is in the bathroom. I guess I have some sort of strange talent for knowing when people are in the bathroom. If only I could harness it for the good of mankind."

Book Reports Will Be Really, Really Good

Someday, you'll be explaining to a bored teenager how tough life was when you were a kid: "Hey, when we had to do a book report on *Moby Dick* we couldn't just load the Monarch Notes CD-ROM, block and copy a few sections, search and replace a couple of terms to avoid plagiarism, jazz it up in Quark, run off thirty presentation copies to bring in along with a laserdisc of the movie to show on the projection laptop. No, we had to walk five miles through the snow to the mall and actually buy a hard copy of the Monarch Notes."

The San Francisco Giants Will Have a Disappointing Season

Not really a consequence of the Digital Revolution, but nevertheless a pretty good prediction.

Disney Will Open Analog World

In about fifty years, Analog World will offer young and old a chance to experience the clumsy but endearing information tools of the twentieth century, combining educational displays—among them a mock math class where "students," complete with pocket protectors, take an algebra test using nothing but pencil, paper, and their brains—with a Rides Section, "where the Slide Rule Water Slide rules!"

Patience? Forget It

If you think television commercials have shortened our attention span, just wait until personal computing has had a few more years. Already we're dissatisfied if it takes our computer more than five seconds to launch a program that, just a decade ago, would have boggled our minds. Once the telephone, television set, radio, and game board have all been subsumed by the computer, almost every significant transaction we attempt will take less than a second to develop.

As a result, anything that takes longer than a second or two won't be able to capture our attention. Speeches, advertisements, even friendly greetings will be abbreviated to compensate for increased impatience. Today's political sound bytes will become tomorrow's State of the Union addresses, and candidates for office will campaign on platforms comprised entirely of buzzwords. If this further reduces political discourse to absurdity, it will make for more entertaining presidential debates:

Question: **Taxes?**
Candidate 1   Bad!
Candidate 2   Necessary!
Candidate 3   Awful!

Question: **Scandal?**
Candidate 1   Bad!

Candidate 2	Necessary!
Candidate 3	Awful!

Question:	**Experience?**
Candidate 1	Lots!
Candidate 2	Unnecessary!
Candidate 3	Some!

Question:	**Conclusion?**
Candidate 1	Me!
Candidate 2	Me!
Candidate 3	No, me!

(Post-debate analysts will criticize Candidate 3 for being long-winded.)

This Country Will Go to Hell in a Handbasket

One of these days, after everyone in the United States has a computer connected to the Internet, someone will come up with the bright idea of instituting computer voting. Instead of having to make the almost superhuman effort of actually finding and using a voting booth, Americans will be able to simply log on from home to cast their votes. The result? Voter turnout will approach 95 percent, and Alicia Silverstone will be elected President.

So What's the Conclusion?

The key to better living through computers is keeping one simple fact in mind:

Everyone wants your money.

It's true. Netscape wants your money. Microsoft wants your money.
Apple doesn't just want your money, it *needs* your money. Cable
companies and phone companies are at each other's throats, fight-
ing for the right to ask for your money.

This isn't a bad thing; in fact it's a good thing. This is business, the
free market at work and it's a beautiful thing. But never forget that:

Everyone wants your money.

You're wondering why I repeat myself. I do so because it's easy to
forget this little fact as you try to navigate the wonder that is cyberspace. Constantly bombarded by new terms and ideas, foreign
phrases, operations, and applications, it's easy to start thinking
that you're just not capable of getting it. You've been hiding your
discomfort and ignorance from your friends and family, while trying
to master just one of the countless computer crazes that seems to
be sweeping the country. At the same time you've been desperately
searching for at least one acquaintance who has less on the ball
than you. And each day you're visited by that nagging doubt: *Maybe
I'm just not good enough for all this stuff.*

That's when you have to remember just one little fact:

Everyone wants your money.

Because if your money is good enough, you are. If you don't get it,
don't buy it. You're in charge here, not the guys who make all this
computer crap. It's not as if you need any of this stuff to go on living—when you get right down to it, the entire trillion-dollar Digital
Revolution is built on something that is essentially an accessory. If
you don't want to give these people your money, you don't have to.
If you don't like how long it takes to load a Web page, instead of

wondering how long it will be before you can afford that faster, zippier new modem—turn the computer off and go for a walk. Drop your Internet provider, dump the browsing software, and don't give it a second thought. If you can write what you need on your 10-year-old 286, there's no reason to feel rotten because you haven't the faintest idea what it means to run a macro. If you're satisfied reading an in-flight magazine, there's no reason to get a multimedia laptop for some heavy *Rebel Assault* action during the fifteen minutes of flight time they actually allow you to run your computer.

Of course, everyone involved in the computer industry—software and hardware dealers and manufacturers, programmers, computer "journalists," and even some authors—disagree with the above. They do everything they can to get you excited about computers, and to make you believe that unless you sign on for a full hitch in the Digital Army, you're not doing your duty as a citizen. You're holding up the great sociological changes that will be wrought by the Digital Revolution. You're a *slacker*. But they're only saying that because:

They want your money.

Remember: their livelihoods depend on you. They will do everything in their power to convince you that you need what they're selling. If you like what they're selling, buy it! But if you don't like it, don't buy it. Chances are, they'll figure out what you will buy, and make *that* instead, like a cheap SIMM chip. Who knows, we might even end up with a color monitor that's actually smaller than a Honda Civic.

Afterword

What can I say? Personal computers are here to stay, so you might as well make the most of it. If you currently own a computer, you already know there's no going back. And if you're just thinking of getting a computer, remember this: he who hesitates is lost. Take the plunge. Join the rest of the wired world. Buy a computer.

Mine's for sale.

Appendix A:

The FAQ (Frequently Asked Questions) for This Book

Q. *What's a FAQ?*
A. I just told you. Frequently Asked Questions.

Q. *How is FAQ pronounced?*
A. It rhymes with *hack*.

Q. *Who determines when a question is asked frequently?*
A. Some guy.

Q. *How can you have a FAQ for a book that just came out?*
A. Next question.

Q. *What is a FAQ for?*
A. A FAQ is compiled by authoritative sources on a particular topic, in order to establish a first line of information for neophytes. For example, the FAQ for Milk Drinkers would include the question "Will anything bad happen if I open the wrong side of the carton?" It would also supply an answer to the question.

Appendix A: The FAQ for This Book

Q. *Will anything bad happen if I open the wrong side of a milk carton?*

A. Sorry, wrong FAQ.

Q. *What's the difference between an official FAQ and an unofficial FAQ?*

A. An official FAQ is written by a representative of that newsgroup, forum, or chat channel. The answers it provides therefore carry the weight of authority. (Just how much authority is required to write a FAQ about découpage is debatable.) An unofficial FAQ is written by anyone who thinks he knows something about the subject, or by someone who is bitter at having lost the election for newsgroup president. The term *unofficial* does not mean that there is anything interesting, scandalous, or prurient about the FAQ; it is just as dull as the official FAQ.

Q. *Are FAQs useful?*

A. Have you learned nothing from this book? No, FAQs are not useful. Although they contain useful information, no one ever reads them. Nobody wants to discover that his informed, considered, timely question has already been asked countless times by hordes of other hapless morons.

Q. *There are countless computer how-to books on the market today, but they all seem to be aimed at dummies. Why is this?*

A. People would rather be called stupid than confused. To admit that you're merely perplexed by something implies that, with a shove in the right direction, you'll be able to figure out what you're doing. Claiming you're an idiot or a dummy entitles you to a lifetime of support on any subject. This is why you will never see a book entitled *Windows for Smart, Attentive People*, whereas *Windows for People Who Suspect They Are in a Persistent, Conscious, Vegetative State* is due out next month.

198

Q. *Is there a FAQ for every newsgroup or Web forum?*
A. All but one. The newsgroup alt.game-show.jeopardy! doesn't have a FAQ. It does, however, have an OQA (pronounced Oh-Kwa), or list of Oft Questioned Answers.

Q. *Do you honestly believe that last bit was funny?*
A. No. That last bit was just padding.

Q. *What's the best part about a FAQ?*
A. The disclaimer. After thirty-seven pages of helpful answers and earnest advice, any FAQ worth its salt adds a line or two mentioning that the author assumes no responsibility, since he really has no idea what he's talking about and, in fact, made up most of the answers.

Q. *How is that any different from the disclaimer in this book?*
A. Next question.

Q. *How can I procure a list of most frequently requested FAQs?*
A. You can't. You have been eaten by a grue.

Appendix B:

Computing Complaints

Personal computing, like any other large-scale sociological event, has given rise to a distinct set of physical and mental ailments related to the computer. Due to the tremendous speed with which PCs captured public attention, authorities have yet to come up with definitive classifications of these ailments. The American Medical Association has, however, compiled a working list of these complaints. They have graciously allowed it to be published, with the understanding that the ailments described are not yet recognized by medical authorities, so there's no reason for everybody to start suing each other over them.

Tetris-head

A form of insomnia resulting from playing a computer game (especially the arcade type) too long, too close to bedtime. Patients, upon closing their eyes, begin to see manifestations of game pieces floating in the dark, and feel compelled to arrange them according to the rules of the game to which they belong. Variations of Tetris-head include:

Doom-Brain, in which any slight noise convinces the sufferer that a hideous mutant is lurking somewhere nearby;

Panic in the Cranium, in which the patient displays the unshakable and irrational belief that Erika Eleniak is really a fine actress.

Scavengitis

Another game-related mental illness, arising from overplaying Leisure Suit Larry–type games. Sufferers, when confronted with a minor, everyday problem, attempt to solve the problem by collecting odd objects from diverse locations. In the archetypal case, patient Harry O., finding a restaurant not yet open, tried to gain access by:

1. picking a tulip from a public garden,

2. stealing a knife from a hardware store,

3. cutting a buttonhole in his jacket with the knife,

4. putting the tulip in the buttonhole,

5. presenting himself at the restaurant as the new maitre d'.

Frustrated in his attempt, the patient climbed into a nearby dumpster and began rooting through the debris, muttering "Hint book, hint book!"

Baywatch Disease

People with this malady suffer under the compulsion to save constantly. Whether working on a spreadsheet, database, or word proc-

essing file, they cannot resist the impulse to save their file every time they make the smallest change. Sometimes this is the result of a tragic loss of data earlier in the patient's life; treatment begins with the discovery of the sad event. Acute sufferers not only save every time they make a change, but save to a new file as well.

Unger's Complaint

These unfortunates cannot tolerate the existence of a nonessential file on their hard drive. Most of their computing time is spent not on work, but on policing their memory, deleting files like read.me, and defragmenting and optimizing their disks. They experience an abnormal satisfaction at watching the onscreen depiction of the hard-drive as it is being optimized; many actually cheer each time a block is moved to a new location. A note of caution: the appearance of any files with a .TMP extension has been known to drive Unger's sufferers into a homicidal frenzy.

Appendix C:

Music Credits

For some reason, programmers get to list the music that they played while writing the code that just cross-linked every file in your root directory. I think this sort of thing is a good idea, not just in publishing but in everyday life. How many times in your life have you done something incredibly stupid, only to have someone ask "What the hell were you thinking?" Rather than stand there and shrug, you could say "Frankly, I was thinking about Michael Stipe and Natalie Merchant singing 'To Sir, with Love' to Bill Clinton." Everyone would understand, ask you not to think about that again, and suggest some sensible music to have in your head—say, Elvis Costello.

Anyway, my inspiration during the grueling authorship process was supplied by the following artists, usually found at random by spinning the dial of a walkman perched next to the keyboard of my computer:

"I Can't Stand Up for Falling Down"	Elvis Costello and the Attractions
"A Nightingale Sang in Berkeley Square"	Bobby Darin
"No One in the World"	Anita Baker

Music Credits

"Every Time You Walk in
  the Room"   Pam Tillis
"Interstate Love Song"   Stone Temple Pilots
"I Have Dreamed"   Nancy LaMott
"Bow Wow Woof Woof How
  Annoying"   The Dog Downstairs
"Meow Meow We're Bored" Vera & Rosie

. . . and, because it takes about half a second for my hand to get from the keyboard to the dial of the radio, half a second of the following selections:

"Lady of Spain"   Eddie Fisher
"Free as a Bird"   The "Beatles"
Anything by . . .   Garth Brooks
Theme from "Friends" The Rembrandts

Glossary

Bit. The basic unit in sketch comedy.

Byte. An 8-bit unit; e.g., a half-hour special.

Two Bits. A quarter.

Two-Bit. A half-hour special on Fox.

Chip. Third child of engineer Steve Douglas; stepbrother to Ernie.

CPU. Central processing unit; a computer's mathematical control center.

C3PU. Your joke here.

External. Breakable.

Internal. Broken.

Initial Font. In a word processing program, the font used in any new file.

Allen Font. In a CBS program, the guy behind the Candid Camera.

If. Synonym for *when*, as in *if* you are having trouble, *if* for some reason the software doesn't work, *if* your new device wipes out your hard drive, *if* you curse the day the personal computer was built.

GIGO. Garbage In, Garbage Out.

GIGOT. 1962 Jackie Gleason film proving the truth of GIGO.

Hacker. An intrusive computer technician, often bearing a user name in direct contrast to his actual personality ("Cybermaster" rather than "Schmuck from Queens") specializing in making unwarranted entries into other computer systems.

Lunger. An unpleasant dinner companion; Doc Holliday.

Lurker. An attractive, albeit silent, forum or newsgroup member.

Glossary

Multi-tasking. The ability to perform simultaneous operations.

"True" multi-tasking. The ability to perform simultaneous operations, and we're not kidding this time.

"Cross-My-Heart-and-Hope-to-Die" Multi-tasking. The ability to perform simultaneous operations—honest to goodness. No, really. Come on, stop laughing. We mean it this time. It's true. *Please* stop laughing.

Menu Bar. An area, usually found at the top of the screen, containing a menu of program or application options.

Bar Menu. Buffalo wings or mozzarella sticks.

Plug-In. Helper Web applications that come tantalizingly close to doing something neat right before crashing your computer.

Paradigm Shift. Digital expression equivalent to "yadda-yadda-yadda."

Scroll Arrow. Native American character on "F Troop."

UPS. Commercial laboratory used to test component fragility.

URL. The sound your stomach makes after too long at the computer.

Version. A semantic trick used by software companies to escape responsibility for ever finishing a project.

Virtual. Anything whose technology is "almost-but-not-quite," but whose price is "right there."

About the Author

Robert P. Libbon has pounded stakes with the Big Apple Circus, spilled blood for Penn & Teller, and breathed fire for the movie *Annie*. His computing experience is informed by two beliefs: 1) that personal computing is "the greatest thing since sliced bread," and 2) that sliced bread is vastly overrated. Libbon lives in New York City with his wife, Janet, and their two cats, Rosie and Vera.